Addiction and Alcoholism Recovery Skills

For Women

Simple Strategies

and Workbook Exercises

To Get Sober, Get Happy

and Prevent Relapse

By Kate Lewis

Table of Contents

Introduction

Hey there, I'm Kate. You might be wondering why a square looking, forty-something-year-old mom from a happy, sunny place like California is writing a book about sobriety. There is a saying that alcoholism and addiction do not discriminate. It doesn't care if you are rich or poor, tall or short, look like a square or look like a dirtbag; and it most certainly doesn't care if you are a man or a woman. So, if you are thinking "why me?", it is actually more like "why *not* you?". We all have crosses to bear (i.e. tough stuff we have to learn to live with), and this is one of yours. It is one of mine too. Alcoholism/addiction is rampant, and you are *so awesome* for wanting to do better for yourself and actually taking the steps to get there.

A handful of things before we get started:

1. There are certain traumas that women are more prone to than men when alcohol and drugs are involved. I won't be touching on them explicitly in this book, because they could be huge triggers for some, but I want to acknowledge first and foremost that if this has been your experience, I see you, and I know you are a fighter. It has taken you an amazing amount of strength to be able to open this book and start reading.

2. My story involves large amounts of alcohol (and a lot, I mean… A LOT of pot), so the examples I provide will be centered around alcohol and alcoholism, but the fundamental despair and all-around awfulness we feel, no matter what the substance of choice is, is quite similar, and the strategies we

can use to overcome it are the same. The tools I outline in this book will apply whether your issue was alcohol, meth, huffing paint, shopping… Whatever it is, you are good to go with this book. If you put these strategies into action, you will STAY sober.

3. There are many tips and tools in this book. If you are serious about your sobriety, take it all in at a pace where each piece of advice has time to sink in so that you can implement them. The workbook exercises will help with this. I want you to *actually* put pen to paper. I put my all into this book. My hope is that you do the same.

4. The path to getting sober is not one size fits all. While I encourage you to at least try all of the suggestions outlined in this book, odds are they won't all feel right to you. Take what works, modify it if needed, and if something simply doesn't seem to be useful, then leave it alone. Remember, it is important to distinguish feelings of stubbornness about not wanting to try something, from actually trying something and realizing it is not helpful.

5. The path to sobriety is also not linear. The strategies in this book are simple, and when put to use, they will keep you sober and get you happy, but you may need time to practice them and learn them well enough to use them properly as your weapons against temptations. So… if you relapse, you HAVE NOT FAILED. It took some time between my decision that I wanted to quit for myself (because ultimately, we can't quit for anyone but ourselves) and when I had my last drink. That is how it is for most people. Pick yourself up and keep fighting, damn it.

6. I won't bore you with tales of wild nights, rock bottoms and shitshow moments. That will not be helpful to you and could even be triggering. Be on the lookout for a memoir if you want the spectacle of all of that. Instead, I'm

here to share my roadmap to sobriety that's as real as it gets. No sugar-coating, no judgment—just honest insights and practical tools to help you kick alcohol to the curb for good and reclaim your power. *One moment at a time.*

Let's dive in.

Kate Lewis

Gratitude Where There Is None

NOTHING NEW CAN COME INTO YOUR LIFE UNLESS YOU ARE GRATEFUL FOR WHAT YOU ALREADY HAVE.

- MICHAEL BERNARD

It's Day One of Getting Sober

Every bone and muscle in your body aches. Your head is throbbing and the withdrawal symptoms or hangover from not having a fix in the past eight hours since you woke up this morning are kicking into high gear. Unfortunately, this is the easy part. Once we start to feel physically better, space frees up in our brains to start thinking about everything we have been drowning out with booze and drugs. The mental anguish we experience thinking about our wrongdoings is far more painful than pounding headaches and achy muscles; and then we relapse. It feels unbearable, we say F-it, we drink or use, and we are back to square one. Let's break that painful cycle and talk about how we can start stringing sober days together without saying F-it.

Everything Sucks – Or at Least it Feels Like it Sucks

I promised you a realistic guide in the introduction and here it is: Step one – feel the shittiness. When I was trying to get sober, I wished so much for a magic pill or a switch that "clicked" for me just like in those rom coms where the guy has that "ah-ha" moment and suddenly knows exactly what to do to get the girl that is totally out of his league. On day one (every single one of my "day ones" in fact) it was nothing like that, and I had no magic pill. If anything, I'd felt like I was making a huge mistake, that everything was too hard and honestly, like I'd bitten off more than I could chew. Staying sober literally felt impossible. Step one for me was feeling everything… everything that I had suppressed while getting drunk, all of the emotions, bills, and conversations with myself that I had been avoiding. They were all waiting for me to put down the bottle. Although my experience is my own, I feel it's safe to say, it might feel the same way for you too. So, my first bit of advice would be to feel it all, *but don't stay there.*

We'll talk more in Chapter 6 about how to face the damage done while you were under the influence, but let's focus first in this chapter and the chapters leading up to that on how to **not** run straight back to the bottle (or pipe, or needle, or, or, or…) the moment the booze wears off and the pile of problems you have acquired comes into focus.

Gratitude

If someone, anyone, even the person I loved most in this world, were to tell me on day one to *find gratitude in the present moment,* I might've strangled them. Went for their neck right then and there in a crazed and debilitating rage. Even now a part of me feels like it would have been justified; remembering how much my bones ached, my head throbbed and how even walking myself to the toilet seemed like a half marathon, and the other half was getting myself back into bed. It sucked and I was certain that there was nothing good about it.

I remember sitting in my bed on day one, gritting my teeth together, wondering how this was ever going to work. Shame-ridden with the tidal wave of reality checks flooding my brain, I rolled over in my bed out of frustration only to find a small journal and a pen that had been stuck between the headboard and my mattress for who knows how long. Weird things get in weird places when you're consistently wasted. I ripped open the notebook and I started to write (in between shakes and muscle cramps) **every single thing that absolutely SUCKED about the present moment.** I wrote about how the trash was still full, how the dishes in the sink were (still) dirty, and how I had no clean underwear. I scribbled down how awful I felt not only about the things I'd done when I was piss drunk, but about how many of the people who loved me tried to get me sober before I was ready. I wrote a lot about how much it hurt to hurt them and about the feeling of impending doom that I just couldn't shake.

Before I knew it, I had filled up four pages in this little journal and that was the first thing that day that felt even moderately *good*. It was then and there I realized that this was a way to let things go, one complaint at a time.

I also remembered all of those irritating moments in the past that I had scoffed at when I was told to be grateful for what I have. I thought to myself, "what do I have to lose?" So I wrote down three things: my legs (they helped me walk and life would be much harder in a wheelchair), my pillow (sleeping – or being passed out – wouldn't be nearly as comfortable without it), and that I hadn't been fired yet (I was hanging on by a thread though!).

I wrote three things down every day for months. A few weeks after I started I could almost physically feel my brain shifting from negative to positive thinking. Cut to six months later and you'd find me in my kitchen, on my knees, in tears, over how fortunate and privileged I was to have a *microwave*. Practicing gratitude is incredibly powerful, and I was eating my words for saying I didn't need it. It is an absolute MUST. If you do only one thing that I recommend in this book, it should be this. (Hopefully you don't feel like strangling me now. If so, I can't say I blame you.).

BONUSES

I put an extra something together for you so you can easily get started on your daily gratitude practice. Also included is a guide on how to get out of a bad living situation and a guide on getting good sleep in early recovery. Download them by scanning the QR code or visiting: www.myhappysoberlife.com

The Done List

On that first day, I had written down just about every single complaint I had about my current situation, my life, my past, my goal of sobriety and then on the flipside, what I was grateful for. It slowly became clear that many of my complaints were actually an overflowing list of to-dos. It was like my brain was keeping a hidden catalog of how many things needed to get done, adding to the subconscious overwhelm I felt when I finally got sober. I realized that if I could write my to-dos, I could also write what I had gotten done that day. I kept it really simple. I wrote down things like how I woke up and didn't immediately take a drink, then how I took myself to the bathroom, how I took a shower and washed my hair. I flipped the switch and started patting myself on the back for tiny accomplishments, even deliberately telling myself I did a great job at combing my hair and that I was going to do the best job I've ever done at putting on my sweats. All of these things were added to **the done list.** When we make a point to congratulate ourselves for getting things done and practicing gratitude, it puts our brains into a positive feedback loop; something we will go into more detail on soon.

When we focus on our gratitude, the tide of disappointment goes out and the tide of love rushes in.

-Kristin Armstrong

Throw Away the Jameson

I'm not going to say that it still wasn't incredibly difficult to get through my day sober, but having the done list gave me a glimmer of positivity – something that I hadn't felt in many years. Now it was time to clear the house of any and all temptations. I started with the bottles in my kitchen, then the stray airport-sized mini bottles in my purse. It finally came to the bottle of Jameson tucked under my bed. The last one.

I held the deep green colored bottle in my hand, took one good look, and threw it in the plastic trash can I'd been toting around the house. To this day, I do not keep any alcohol in my home. No cooking wine. No "just in case I have guests" bottles. Nothing. I have no business having it in my possession.

I went back to my journal and wrote down all of my accomplishments on that first day, and the second day, and for months to come. Just like I did with my gratitude list. I felt more and more proud and fulfilled as time went on and the cravings, ever so slowly, became easier to bear.

Rewiring Your Brain – A Positive Feedback Loop

It turns out that positive thinking, AKA the feeling of gratitude, can help rewire your brain. By looking on the bright side, or the "done-list" side of things, you can positively condition yourself and your thought process to find the joy in your struggles; *thus creating a positive feedback loop that gets stronger every time you look on the bright side.* Remember how I said I could actually FEEL my brain switching from negative to positive thinking?

Research has shown that practicing gratitude not only influences our psychological well-being, but also significantly affects our relationships and other interpersonal dynamics (Grant, Gino, & Hofmann, 2015). By embracing gratitude, we can foster deeper connections with others and enhance our quality of life, making it a valuable tool for personal growth and happiness. Although I'll dive more into this in Chapter 2, the fact of the matter is that finding gratitude in the present moment could be the deciding factor of whether you just get sober or **stay sober in the long run.**

Negative thoughts are often a precursor to relapse, so it is important to practice flipping the script as often as possible.

Key Takeaways:

It Starts with Gratitude: Gratitude is the foundation of sobriety. By rewiring your brain to focus on the positive, you can transform your mindset and create a positive feedback loop.

Let Go of the Guilt: By allowing ourselves to feel the guilt of our past-doings we're opening the door to healing and allowing ourselves to walk through it.

It's Normal to Struggle, But Don't Wallow: It's normal to struggle and doubt yourself, especially in the early days of sobriety – feel all the feelings but don't sit and wallow in your past so long that you put yourself at risk of relapse and forget to live your present.

Action Items:

The Pros and Cons

Write a list of pros and cons with one catch – for every con you write it has to come with a pro perspective. For example, a "con" could be "I hate how sobriety feels" but the alternative "pro" would be "I know that in the long run, getting sober will help me learn to love myself."

The Done List

Create a "Done List" of things you've already accomplished on a given day. Start with incredibly small items like "I washed my hair" or "I went to the bathroom" and level up as you go. Review it at the end of the day, taking note of how much you accomplished.

The 3/30 Challenge

Write down three gratitudes each day for a total of thirty days. At the beginning of the thirty days write a short paragraph on if this exercise could have a positive effect on your mindset. At the end of the thirty days, review your previous answer and compare it with how you feel after the challenge is complete.

In the Next Chapter:

In the next chapter, we'll talk about the baby steps that create a bigger foundation for us to thrive in the long run. We'll also talk about how we can create more manageable, bite-sized goals, even amidst an intense urge to drink or use drugs.

The Pros and Cons List

Write a list of pros and cons with one catch – for every con you write it has to come with a pro perspective. For example, a "con" could be "I hate how sobriety feels" but the alternative "pro" would be "I know that in the long run, getting sober will help me learn to love myself." Another example could be, "I'm too tired to exercise" whereas the "pro" would be, "exercise will give me more energy and improve my mood."

Con (e.g. I hate how sobriety feels)	Pro (e.g. In the long run my life will improve)

References:

Grant, A. M., Gino, F., & Hofmann, D. A. (2015). *Reversing the Extramarital Effect: The Power of Gratitude.* Psychological Science, 26(12), 1750-1758.

One Minute At A Time

SUCCESS IS A STAIRCASE, NOT A DOORWAY.

-DOTTIE WALTERS

Don't Stop Climbing

In almost every addiction recovery confessional, video, or seminar, there's always that pivotal moment where the speaker talks about how things simply started working out and how everything just magically fell into place. Just like that "a-ha" moment I mentioned in the first chapter. It almost seems like for these people there was one miraculous moment where they caught a break and everything was just peachy. In actuality, it is all of the tiny micro-battles you fight every day, when you're desperate to make it through just one minute, one hour, one day, without drinking that result in that beautiful moment. I was four and a half months sober when I had mine. It was the day after I had my last craving for alcohol. I have not had even one teeny tiny urge to drink alcohol since that day. It wasn't that there was something I did any differently that *day*. There was something special about the effort I had put in for the year and a half (or 547ish days) that I had been working on getting and staying sober that led up to that day.

In this chapter, we'll talk about the time, effort, and evaluation of our daily urges that allow us to eventually have our moment in the sun; the practices we set into place to get through our days and the small victories where we feel proud of ourselves for achieving our daily goals and withstanding our cravings as we climb (and sometimes army crawl) up the staircase to lasting sobriety. Moments we'll later realize piled on top of each other to help us finally reach true freedom from the shackles and chains of our addictions.

One Minute At A Time

When we hear stories from others in the recovery community about overcoming addiction we often hear phrases that are true for many people, like the common encouragement – *just take it one day at a time*. It's pivotal to have a community to lean on during your journey to recovery (something we'll talk more about in the next chapter), and to be able to relate to each other about having had a common struggle, but I want to acknowledge that triggers look different for everyone, and your story is uniquely your own. You could be fine during the week but think it's impossible not to binge drink at parties during the weekends. You could feel desperate for a drink only in the evenings, or need to sip throughout the day, every day – never totally drunk, never totally sober. Regardless of the circumstance, some days we all feel like it's impossible to go even one more day without drinking or using, making the ever-present advice *just take it one day at a time*, still not enough, because even thinking about the entire day ahead can be too overwhelming. *That's when I started taking things one* **minute, or action,** *at a time.*

I realized that to be able to focus on the present moment and not the day ahead, the most effective strategy for me was to narrate my every move, from the moment I woke up to the moment I went to bed. Not out loud, of course… that would be weird. Unless you are alone. I may have recited it out loud when I was alone.

Here is an example of the script: "My alarm is going off… ok, I need to open my eyes and turn it off. Now what? I need to sit up, ok, now stand up… that wasn't so bad, deep breath, walk to the bathroom, exhale… nailed it… pull my pants down, sit on the toilet, pee, wipe, stand up, pull up pants, flush. Ok, now I need to brush my teeth and I'm going to brush my teeth and I'm going to do a damn good job of it, pick up my toothbrush, pick up my toothpaste" and so on and so forth.

Doing this occupied my brain in such a way that it became extremely difficult for intrusive thoughts to get in and take over the narrative, and then my actions (like drinking because I got stuck in a PTSD moment thinking about that time my boyfriend died right in front of my eyes).

If I noticed myself in a shame spiral about the guys whose names I didn't remember, or future tripping about how my boss is going to fire me for calling out sick three times last week, I would immediately start to narrate what I was doing in that moment to get myself to focus on showing up right now and doing the next right thing. It wasn't until a year or two into my sobriety that I was told that I was actually practicing mindful meditation to stay in the present moment. Like what Buddhist monks do to seek peace. My reaction: "haha! no shit?!"

Those Darn Cravings Though

I used to feverishly pace and wring my hands trying to get through cravings without giving in. They can come on like a chokehold from The Rock, and I wasn't quite practiced enough yet at my Buddhist enlightenment to ALWAYS be able to snap myself out of a craving and into the present moment in the beginning.

In therapy, there is an exercise that is commonly known as *urge surfing*. A tool that aids in stopping a compulsion by simply allowing ourselves to observe an urge without judgment. Research shows that those who can sit with their uncomfortable feelings, bring mindfulness to those moments, and resist the pang of a strong urge are more well off to manage their feelings of anxiety and depression, which are SO common for people in addiction recovery. (Costa et al., 2021).

The first time I tried it, I sat in my kitchen chair and stared at the clock, watching the seconds pass as I tried to resist the urge to go buy alcohol. I could feel my nails digging into the palms of my hands, which were balled up into sweaty fists. Another minute passed, then another… After about five minutes of doing absolutely nothing, but sitting with the craving – I started to *relax*. I started to unclench my jaw, allowed my hands to rest peacefully in the middle of my lap, and took several deep breaths. It was NOT any easier to get through the cravings the first few times I tried this, but every time, I would purposefully sit down and close my eyes, recognize my urge, and sit with it. I got better with practice (you can't get good at anything without practice, right?) and soon enough cravings went from being like a chokehold from The Rock, to a chokehold from Judge Judy; still mean, but not nearly as strong. Now, like I said before, I don't even have them anymore.

H.A.L.T.

Cravings tend to come on when we aren't feeling at peace, and let's face it, that happens often if not always in the first days, weeks, or even months of sobriety. Another incredibly powerful tool that is useful to have at hand and that is well-known and widely used in the recovery community is the acronym H.A.L.T. If we are having a craving, or are otherwise feeling on edge, we can ask ourselves, am I **H**ungry, **A**ngry, **L**onely or **T**ired? And then remedy ourselves accordingly. When we do, we feel *much* better. Most are fairly straightforward, aside from the **A**. Managing our anger takes practice and we can do that by finding support through our community and professional help. We will touch on this more in later chapters.

Key Takeaways:

Luck Is the Result of Consistent Effort: Recovery is all about acknowledging and embracing the "minute-at-a-time" moments, not expecting a random stroke of luck to make things easier.

One Minute at a Time: By focusing on getting through one more minute or action at a time, you can keep yourself busy in the present moment, which will keep you from feeling depressed about the past or anxious about the future; things that all too often lead to relapse.

There's Power in Perspective: Take a moment each day to acknowledge your wins, no matter how small they may seem. Understand that setbacks are a natural part of the journey and instead of dwelling on them, focus on what you can learn and how you can grow from the experience. Once we shift our mindset and find gratitude in the present moment we can transform how we view and navigate the challenges of becoming sober.

More Practice, Less Judgment: Consistently working on controlling our urges through observation without judgment allows us to reduce anxiety and increase our ability to make it through those difficult moments when we have cravings and feel triggered.

Action Items:

Celebrate the "Little Wins"

Note and celebrate each minute of sobriety as a victory and acknowledge the strength it took to overcome the urge to drink. Each time, make a note of the date, time, and any comments you'd like to add in your notebook or notes app. At the end of the month, go back and acknowledge all of the little wins for that month.

Practice Urge Surfing

Start incorporating urge surfing into your daily routine. When you feel the urge to drink or use drugs, pause, observe the sensation without judgment, and allow it to pass. Keep a journal to track your progress and reflect on what triggered the urge. This will allow you to be more mindful of your triggers and thus, more capable of managing them.

Mindful Moments

Practice mindfulness exercises to stay present in the moment. Take a few moments each day to focus on your surroundings and sensations, letting go of past regrets and future worries. Narrate what you're doing to stay focused. Create a weekly goal of doing this at least once a day, increasing the frequency as you achieve your weekly goals.

Seek Support

Surround yourself with a community that understands your journey and can offer guidance and encouragement. Reach out to a therapist or support group to explore additional coping strategies and connect with others on a similar journey. More about this in the next chapter.

In the Next Chapter:

In the next chapter, we'll focus on improving the present moment by engaging in hobbies, finding a community where you feel comfortable expressing yourself, and the importance of prioritizing self-care – especially when you don't feel like doing it.

Urge Surfing Worksheet

In this worksheet, we'll first outline the four stages of urge surfing, then apply them to a particular scenario where you've been tempted to use your substance of choice. Below we've also noted how long each stage lasts.

1. **Trigger (30 seconds to 1 minute)**

   You're confronted with an urge by a person, place, thing or thought that triggers a guttural, emotional response.

2. **Rise (3 minutes)**

   As this emotional response rises, the tension begins to build within your body. You could start anxiously tapping your foot or have a hard time finding a comfortable sitting position.

3. **Peak (1.5 minutes)**

   You reach the pinnacle of the urge and the feeling is *almost inescapable and all consuming*. It feels like all you want in this moment is the thing you cannot have.

4. **Fall (5 minutes)**

   The urge starts to die down and you slowly start to gain control over your breathing, anxiety and any other emotional responses that are triggered.

Urge Surfing Questions:

Think of a scenario where you've been triggered then tempted to use your substance of choice and apply it to the questions below.

My Scenario is:

_____

_____

Stage 1: Trigger

Describe your triggering moment in detail. What was the person, place or thing that initiated your emotional response? Are you alone? Are you with friends? Describe the experience below.

_____

_____

_____

_____

_____

_____

Stage 2: Rise

In this imaginary scenario, how did you react both emotionally and physically? Did your palms get sweaty or did your mouth start to get dry as if you *needed* that sip of alcohol? Describe the build-up below.

_____

_____

_____

_____

_____

_____

Imagine what thoughts were running through your head as the urge built up. What are you telling yourself? What *could* you tell yourself that aligns more with your sobriety?

_____

_____

_____

_____

Stage 3: Peak

You're at the very pinnacle of your urge. What raw emotions are you feeling? What stands out to you the most?

_____

_____

_____

_____

_____

_____

Now, imagine yourself trying to cope with your urge. What do you *want to do* versus what do you think you *should do* to calm yourself down? How did you successfully resist this urge in this imaginary scenario?

_____

_____

_____

_____

_____

_____

Stage 4: Fall

As the urge to use your substance of choice falls, how do you feel? Do you notice yourself unclenching your fists, or taking more calming, deep breaths? How does it feel to resist the urge? Reflect on how you feel proud of yourself (or another positive emotion) for successfully resisting your urge.

_____

_____

_____

_____

_____

_____

Bonus Question:

The next time you're faced with an urge to use your substance of choice – what will you do differently?

_____

_____

_____

_____

_____

_____

References:

Costa, A., Dores, A. R., Costa, D., Levy, A. R., & Antunes, A. M. M. (2021). Health-related quality of life of individuals with different alcohol use patterns: A cross-sectional study. *Alcoholism Treatment Quarterly*, 39(4), 432-451.

Keep Yourself Occupied (Keep Yourself Alive)

KEEP YOURSELF ALIVE, YEAH,

KEEP YOURSELF ALIVE,

. . . . .

HONEY, YOU'LL SURVIVE.

-"KEEP YOURSELF ALIVE" BY QUEEN

A Life We Want to Stay Present For

You made it through another day! But now what? For many of us who are navigating the twists and turns of life in sobriety, the question of "What's next?" can feel overwhelming. Keeping ourselves alive is all well and good but surviving isn't quite living and vice versa.

That's where keeping yourself occupied comes in. Engaging in hobbies, connecting with a supportive community, and prioritizing self-care are like the glue that holds your sobriety together. When you're busy and fulfilled, the temptation to reach for drugs as a coping mechanism slowly fades into the background. In this chapter, we'll focus on creating routines and joining different communities that not only make it harder for us to slip back into active addiction but also make our lives *enjoyable* – a life we want to be present for where we wake up and actually look forward to the day ahead.

Your Life: Starring – You

Think about it like this: you're the star of your own show, and each day presents a new opportunity to shine; but to do so, you need a strong supporting cast (community) and a killer script. This is where hobbies come in. I was really fragile in the early days, so I started small. The first thing I got into was watching stand-up comedy. Some would say that's not a hobby, but I honestly thought of it as art appreciation – it never failed to put a smile on my face, it kept me occupied and it kept me *sober*. It connected me to others, because I started sharing good comics and shows with friends and family, especially when they shared with me that they were feeling down. It made me feel so good when they told me that it helped so much to cheer them up, and then we laughed about some of the jokes together.

Hobbies give you something to look forward to and keep your mind engaged in the present moment. Plus, as you get yourself out there more and more, they're a great way to meet new people who share your interests, and can provide a sense of belonging.

Leveling Up

Just like those 90's arcade games (or Netflix and my couch), we have to start at the bottom. Mario didn't start level one by going to the castle and rescuing Princess Peach, and quite similarly, you shouldn't expect yourself to be thrown into big new hobbies, or significant changes in your routine, and handle things swimmingly.

Leveling Up Isn't Linear

It's also important to recognize that progress isn't always linear. There will be days when you feel like you're back at level one, battling the same demons you thought you had already conquered. But remember, every time you face those challenges head-on, you're gaining points that will eventually help you improve your overall quality of life. So, don't be discouraged by setbacks; embrace them as opportunities for growth, find gratitude where there is none, and keep pushing forward.

Try All the Salt-Water Taffy

Finding a hobby that suits you is like being a kid in a small-town candy store. You see all the colorful barrels filled up with different kinds of salt-water taffy. As a child, I always wished I could try each and every one of them and then come back and pick out just my favorite flavors. Eventually, after many trips, I was able to narrow down that I absolutely adored passionfruit, cotton candy, and Neapolitan, but HATED black licorice and hot cinnamon.

Finding hobbies that work for you is a lot like this — trying a bit of everything to see what you like and dislike. You may realize that you're not a bad painter, but cycling hurts your butt too much; or that yoga makes you feel G-R-E-A-T, but baking bores the heck out of you. As you narrow it down and do more of what you love, you will begin to liberate parts of your spirit that you had been completely disconnected from.

For each taffy you try, you get a lot closer to finding something that you love, until eventually your whole life is filled with things that genuinely bring you joy.

If you are worried about the expense of a new hobby, just think about how much that nightly six-pack set you back and invest even HALF of that amount of money into it — you'll be all set.

Self-Care, a Non-Negotiable

Although we'll talk more about this in Chapter 7, I wanted to note how creating new routines and prioritizing self-care are also critical components of maintaining your sobriety. Just like brushing your teeth or eating food, self-care should be a non-negotiable part of your daily routine. It's also important to recognize the difference between a healthy indulgence that promotes self-care and one rooted in self-sabotage. By taking time to care for yourself, you're setting into motion an affirmation that you deserve to be loved and pampered… by YOU. So please, create a spa day for yourself in your bathroom (or an actual spa if you can afford it), sleep in on a Sunday, or have a good cry because letting yourself process your emotions is self-care too. Lemme tell you, engaging in a super healthy helping of self-care got me through some of my *meanest* cravings.

The Proof Is in the Pudding

Have you ever noticed that the first couple of days in a new routine or hobby are the hardest? I find this especially true with exercise if I haven't done it in a while. One of the most difficult things to do is simply *starting,* but as you chip away it gets easier and easier. Research from the National Center for Biotechnology Information shows that after some time, routines become solidified in your brain, making them easier to follow the longer you do them. So, by staying consistent with the things that bring you joy, and prioritizing your well-being, you're not only strengthening your sobriety, you're also laying the foundation for a happier, healthier life.

Recent research by Bos, Kuiper, and Van Raalten (2018) explored how our brains form habits and remember various things from our day. They came to the same conclusion; that when we repeatedly do something, like following a routine or engaging in a hobby, our brain strengthens the connections related to those actions, making them easier to do over time without having to think too much about it. As we *level up,* these repetitive actions get logged into our brains as memories, further strengthening our new positive routine until it eventually becomes second nature.

Recent studies have also shown that engaging in activities that promote well-being, such as exercise, mindfulness meditation, and social interaction, can have a profound impact on mental health and emotional well-being (Bos et al., 2018). So don't be afraid to try new things, embrace change, and prioritize self-care – your future self will thank you for it. **You *deserve* to live a beautiful, meaningful life.**

Joining a Community

You ARE A People Person

I know you might be thinking – *I'm not a big group type of person,* or *I like my space and privacy,* or *joining a group isn't for me.* You might not feel comfortable in large groups or joining a community where you don't know anyone *and that's okay.* I, myself, am not exceptionally outgoing, and if I must socialize, I prefer one-on-one or small-group conversations. For me, joining a community felt like another "impending doom" type of task – similar to day one of being sober. It took months before I could choke out "I need help," or worse, "I'm an alcoholic," in front of others without falling apart at the seams. At the time I felt embarrassed and weak, but I now know that asking for help is one of the bravest things anyone can do and I am pretty freaking proud of myself for engaging in that kind of badassery. Talk about leveling up.

The fact is that we *need* people and community, whether we like it or not. It makes us feel like we belong, like we are also needed and that we are part of something important. I highly recommend women's groups to start.

Sharing In Our Shame Makes It Go Away

Early on, before I knew which way was up when I was working on staying sober, I remember confiding in another woman in a recovery group who had agreed to coach me how I had peed on my couch while I was passed out a couple of weeks before. It was so hard to tell her and I felt like a dirty, worthless loser about it… and then she laughed! For two whole seconds I just wanted to crawl away and die (I frequently felt like that at the time). Then she proceeded to say "that only happened to you once?!? I peed on my couch, my best friend's bed, and on the floor after a party at the house of someone I didn't even know!"

This woman was cool in my eyes. She was pretty, fun, nice and had her stuff together. I wanted that for myself so much. The fact that it had happened to her too and she was able to LAUGH about it, gave me so much hope. It was the first time I had felt hope for myself and my existence in a very long time.

If I had never reached out for community, I am sure by now I really would have crawled away and died…

The World Wide Web

Whether you hate it or love it, the internet has opened all sorts of new opportunities to connect with others. It's a perfect first step if you are almost literally crippled by the thought of walking into a community of perfect strangers in person right away. Seriously, go Google "alcohol (or addiction) recovery support group" and be overwhelmed by the amount of options you have at your fingertips.

Don't Knock it Till You Try it

You can engage in discussions, seek advice, or simply lurk in the background until you feel ready to participate. Plus, the beauty of online communities is that they often provide a level of anonymity, allowing you to share your thoughts and experiences without fear of judgment. So if the thought of attending an in-person meeting sends shivers down your spine, consider exploring the vast expanse of the internet for a community that resonates with you. Be safe. There are snakes online, so I'd keep it anonymous until you feel certain you are in the right place.

Key Takeaways:

Join a Community: By joining a community, in-person or otherwise, we're able to receive support, and share our thoughts, feelings, and struggles in a safe space.

Try New Things: Just like trying different flavors of taffy, sometimes we need to try various hobbies until we find one that fits juuuust right. Don't be afraid to try several new things before you find something that sticks. Your future self will thank you for it.

Build a Routine, It's Good For You: Building a solid routine that includes hobbies, community and self-care can be difficult to start but incredibly worth it in the long run. After some time, routines become second nature, thus making them easier to stick to in the long run.

Be Consistent: By consistently engaging in activities that bring you joy and prioritizing your well-being, you're not only strengthening your sobriety but also laying the foundation for a happier, healthier life.

Action Items:

The Community Challenge

Start by joining an online community and leveling up over time, eventually getting to the point where you join an in-person community. Track your progress over time by writing your thoughts and feelings before and after you complete stages 1, 2, and 3.

Try Some Taffy

Set a goal for yourself to try at least one new hobby per week. Take note of how you'll accomplish this goal by writing the details of where the hobby will take place, how you'll map it into your schedule, if you need to rent equipment, and if you need to go to the class at a certain time. By ironing out the details, it's easier to execute your plan and stick to your new routine. Plan it out so that it feels easy to follow through with when the time comes.

Mindful Moments

Practice mindfulness exercises to stay present in the moment. Take a few moments each day to focus on your surroundings and sensations, letting go of past regrets and future worries. Create a weekly goal of doing this at least once a day, increasing the frequency as you achieve your weekly goals.

Seek Support

Surround yourself with a community that understands your journey and can offer guidance and encouragement. Reach out to a therapist or support group to explore additional coping strategies and connect with others on a similar journey.

In the Next Chapter:

In the next chapter, we'll look into what to say when you don't know what to say – specifically when you have to tell your neighbor, friend, or family member that you've stopped drinking. We'll break down the triggers that are associated with the "actually, I've stopped drinking" conversation and how to create solid boundaries when it comes to temptation. At any stage of recovery, it can be an awkward conversation to have, especially when we're met with phrases like *oh c'mon you weren't even that bad* or even worse, having people you know try to goad you into *one little drink*.

The Community Challenge:

Level 1: Explore Various Communities

Explore different types of communities both online and in-person within your neighborhood. Again, I highly recommend starting with women's groups. Reflect on how you feel before you start researching different groups and hobbies. At the end, write about your experience and answer the before and after questions below.

Before you start:

Reflect on your interests and hobbies. What activities bring you joy and fulfillment? Were there any hobbies you used to love and stopped doing because of alcohol or drug addiction? Is there anything that you wanted to try to learn to do but haven't yet? What got in your way?

_____

_____

_____

_____

_____

_____

_____

_____

_____

_____

_____

_____

_____

What are some potential communities or groups you've considered exploring? List them below:

_____

_____

_____

_____

_____

_____

_____

_____

_____

_____

Take action:

Research different types of communities, such as local clubs, online forums, or neighborhood groups. Jot down the ones you have found that look good to you:

Types of Communities	Types of Online Forums	Groups in My Neighborhood

After you're done:

How do you feel about joining a new community now that you have tried it out? Are there any reservations or concerns? Was it more or less difficult to find some that interest you than you thought it'd be? Did you find something you will continue to participate in? If so, why? If not, move on to the next option on your list and try again. Keep trying until something clicks.

_____

_____

_____

_____

_____

_____

_____

_____

_____

_____

Level 2: Join an Online Community

Join an online community for two weeks, 14 days total. Make it a point to interact on a day-to-day basis and do your best to become an active member of the group. Join several online platforms and at the end of the two weeks, report your findings below. Before joining each group, write down your thoughts and feelings, and answer the questions below.

Before joining:

Consider your comfort level with online interactions and social media platforms.

_____

_____

_____

_____

Question: What online communities align with your interests or provide support related to your recovery journey?

_____

_____

_____

_____

_____

_____

_____

Take action:

Sign up for online forums, social media groups, or virtual support networks relevant to your interests or recovery goals.

Name of Group	Type of Group (Forum, Reddit Group, Facebook Community, etc.)	On a scale of 1-10 (10 being the most hopeful) how do I feel about joining this group?

After joining:

How did you feel about joining an online community? Were you excited, nervous, or apprehensive about interacting with others online in the beginning? How do you feel now that you've been interacting in the group for two weeks? What did you like most? What did you dislike?

_____

_____

_____

_____

_____

_____

_____

_____

_____

_____

_____

_____

_____

_____

_____

_____

_____

_____

_____

Level 3: Join an In-Person Sober Community or Support Group:

Join an in-person support group and participate regularly for one month and reflect on your experience. Before you join the group, write down any thoughts or feelings you have and answer the "before" questions, below. After consistently going to meetings for one month, answer the "after" questions and reflect on if it was as difficult as you thought at the beginning of the exercise.

Before joining:

Reflect on your experiences with sobriety and any challenges you've faced. How do you think joining a community could help you accomplish your goal of staying sober? What are some other feelings you have about joining an in-person community?

_____

_____

_____

_____

_____

_____

_____

_____

_____

_____

_____

Have you considered joining a sober community or support group to connect with others on a similar journey? Do you feel reluctant? If so, why? If not, why? Do you feel hopeful? If so, why? If not, why?

_____

_____

_____

_____

_____

_____

_____

_____

_____

Take action:

Explore options for sober communities, such as local Alcoholics Anonymous (AA) or Narcotics Anonymous (NA) meetings, Refuge Recovery meetings, Smart Recovery meetings, virtual support groups, or other specialized recovery programs. Write down the communities you're thinking about joining, below:

Name of Group	Address	Meeting Times and Frequency of Meetings

After joining for one month:

How do you feel about the idea of joining an in-person sober community or support group now? Have you found support and encouragement from connecting with others who understand your experiences? What did you like and what did you dislike? Will you continue? If so, why? If not, move on to the next option and try that one. Keep going until you find something that clicks.

_____

_____

_____

_____

_____

_____

_____

_____

_____

_____

_____

_____

_____

_____

_____

_____

_____

_____

_____

_____

Bonus Level: Engage in Activities that Bring You Joy

Before engaging in new activities:

Think about activities or hobbies that bring you happiness and fulfillment, or that you have often felt compelled to try.

Type of Activity	Why It Brings Me Joy	Other Related Hobbies in This Category

Question: How can you incorporate these activities into your routine to enhance your sense of well-being and connection within the community?

_____

_____

_____

_____

_____

_____

_____

Take action:

Identify activities that align with your interests, such as art, fitness, or outdoor adventures, and make plans to participate in them regularly.

Type of Activity	Location or Address of Activity	Meeting Time for Activity / Plan to Routinely Do This Hobby

After engaging in a new activity or activities for one month:

How do you feel about prioritizing self-care and engaging in activities that bring you joy now? Are you optimistic about the positive impact these activities can have or are having on your overall well-being and recovery journey?

_____

_____

_____

_____

_____

_____

_____

_____

_____

_____

_____

_____

_____

_____

_____

_____

_____

_____

I know we went a little heavy on these exercises and it was purposeful. Active addiction is an incredibly lonely place to be. Some say that it is a disease that WANTS us alone so it can continue to thrive and destroy us. There is another very popular saying that "the opposite of addiction is connection."

By following these steps, you can explore different communities at your own pace, connect with like-minded people (who are therefore obviously super cool), and find support and encouragement on your journey towards a happier, more fulfilling life that is free of the despair that is caused by addiction.

Deep breath… YOU GOT THIS.

References:

Bos, D. J., Kuiper, R. M., & Van Raalten, T. R. (2018). Understanding the role of the ventromedial prefrontal cortex in memory encoding across the lifespan. *The Journal of Neuroscience*, 38(44), 9389-9391.

Lee, S. W., Gerhart, J., Braynen, T., & Bonifas, R. P. (2019). The effects of a regular exercise program on the brain health of pregnant women. *Journal of Clinical Medicine*, 8(4), 451.

What to Say to People When You've Stopped Drinking

TEMPTATION IS THE FEELING WE GET WHEN ENCOUNTERED BY AN OPPORTUNITY TO DO WHAT WE INNATELY KNOW WE SHOULDN'T.

-NEIL STRAUSS

You Weren't THAT Bad...

Well I hate to break it to you but the truth is — you probably were that bad. Most likely much worse than your friends, family members, coworkers or neighbors thought you were. The fact of the matter is that we get *so incredibly good* at hiding the fact that we're tipsy or high and as time goes on, we get better at acting like we're *completely fine.*

Temptation usually comes in through a door that has deliberately been left open.

- Arnold Glasow

The Kasey Catch 22

As hard as it is to hear, some people might want you to fail. They might subtly enable your drinking or using, or outright egg you on in an effort to support or validate their own. These people can be incredibly triggering and we need to talk about them first.

Let me share a story – back when my relationship with alcohol was at its peak, there was this coworker friend of mine, let's call her Kasey. We were the dynamic duo at concerts, the last to leave any party, and our idea of unwinding always involved Jameson shots with IPA backs and a spliff or two along the way. We had bonded over our love for live music, the thrill of the nightlife, and, of course, our shared enthusiasm for a good drink. But then came my decision to sober up. The thought of breaking this news to Kasey felt like gearing up for a heavyweight bout. I honestly wished she would just disappear, because the mere thought of her made me think about how good that first mind-numbing shot always felt (before it led to disaster and/or emotional turmoil, of course). In my mind, I rehearsed the conversation countless times, each scenario ending with a different reaction, none of which felt particularly encouraging. It wasn't just Kasey; it was the anticipation of outing myself as sober to our entire circle of friends.

I practiced my speech in the mirror dozens of times. "I can do this. It's going to be okay." I'd say to myself at the end of every rehearsal. And for the most part, it was okay. The moment of truth came at 12:00 pm on a Tuesday. I had skipped work that Monday, because even though the anxiety was running strong, the physical withdrawal symptoms hadn't totally subsided yet. It was lunchtime and Kasey and friends immediately started discussing which happy hour we wanted to hit after work. Before I could think much about it, I blurted out, "I can't go! I stopped drinking!" It was sudden, it was awkward, and it did not come out the way I had rehearsed AT ALL. Thankfully, one of our friends, always the mother hen of our group, reached over and squeezed my shoulder, offering a simple yet powerful, "Good for you!"

The relief was immediate, almost overwhelming, as everyone else chimed in with their support, their smiles genuine, their eyes kind. Everyone, that is, except Kasey.

Kasey and I had shared more than just a few drinks; we had countless memories tied up in our adventures, from sneaking flasks into concerts to bottomless mimosa brunches after Sunday morning yoga… where I often felt like I was just sweating vodka and breathing through nausea. Her reaction wasn't the proud encouragement I had hoped so much for. Instead, I was met with a look that mixed disbelief with a hint of betrayal. Her laughter cut through the warm bubble of support – "Oh, come ON, Kate. You weren't that bad," she scoffed. The implication hanging heavy in the air. Her words seemed to hang for a moment before one of our friends gently intervened, trying to smooth over the tension. But Kasey wasn't having it. It was obvious she felt like I was pooping on her perpetual party. "You say that now, but we'll see how long this lasts," she half-joked, half-hoped-I-would-continue-to-drink-with-her-probably-to-prove-to-herself-that-she-wasn't-that-bad-either. I wondered how much she ever cared about me, and if she just loved that she didn't have to drink alone, because I ALWAYS joined her. We even *joked* about how much we drank when we weren't even with each other.

The atmosphere shifted, the previously supportive bubble now tainted with an undercurrent of discomfort. I felt a flush of shame, not for my choice, but for causing this rift, however unintentional. "I'm sorry, Kasey, this is just something I need to do for me," I found myself saying, my voice far steadier than I felt. Another friend quickly changed the subject by complimenting the mother hen on her new blouse, a silent agreement to move past the awkwardness.

That moment with Kasey was a turning point, a stark reminder that not everyone would understand or support my journey. But it also highlighted the strength of the support system I hadn't realized I had. As we moved on to discuss our latest bargain finds and complain about how they always seemed to be clothes for work, I couldn't help but feel a little lighter and a bit more confident in my path. Sure, there were challenges ahead, but at that moment, I knew I had at least some of the players on my team rooting for me. I was able to find gratitude in that, and it was a giant relief.

Better Things Ahead

Whatever powerful force you believe in, if any – I think it's safe to say we attract what we put out in the world and when I was an alcoholic, I was not a good friend, so I attracted the same. In the moment I wondered if Kasey ever really cared about me, I also wondered how much I truly cared about her. The thing is, when we fill our circle full of those looking to indulge in the same vices and not feel guilty over it, those people might not have actually been there "as a friend" in the first place. I found out a few weeks after I got sober that Kasey was one of those people. Over time I realized that at the center of our relationship had always been an alcoholic buffer and that without it, I started to really notice the snide remarks, sarcastic comments and subtle looks of envy for *even attempting recovery*. All in all, our addiction was really the only thing we had in common and was what our "friendship" was based on.

I had many friendships like this that I had to step away from. At first it felt really sad, but the longer I stayed sober, the more I realized that relationships that revolved around sloppy *I love you, man* moments and "being there for each other" by helping each other get into a cab safely after puking on the bartender were a huge part of what was keeping me absolutely miserable. This kind of friendship has absolutely nothing on the friendships where we cheer each other on to live our healthiest, happiest, most badass lives by working to make our wildest dreams come true. You really are who you hang with.

I stopped going to happy hour and hanging out with Kasey altogether and instead was introduced to a Monday night women's meeting, Tuesday night yoga, and a hugely entertaining Thursday open mic night at a coffee shop in the Lower Haight. I was about three weeks into my new routine when I stopped to look at myself in the mirror. I realized it was the first time I was able to look myself in the eye in a very long time, which made me well up with tears. Not only that, I felt a bit proud. My skin was clearing up, the bloat in my face was all but gone, and I looked a little bit... *happy*. I smiled at myself, and then just like I did in the microwave moment (see Chapter 1), I cried right then and there. So much so that I had to have a seat.

I realized that I was so grateful and so happy to have started these new routines and I was seeing my hard work paying off. Not only had I cultivated a great group of girlfriends and felt good about taking care of my body and myself, *but that I was worthy of it.* I'll talk more about self-compassion in Chapter 10 but for now, what you need to know is **there are better things ahead.** It totally sucks at first, but if you stick with it and stay strong, life just gets better and better (and better). I PROMISE.

Understanding Your Triggers

Ahh, understanding our triggers. It's what I wish I had known during my conversation with Kasey and something I'd learn to navigate time and time again when it came to talking about how I didn't drink anymore. It's also important to note that **you don't owe anyone an explanation.** I've made the mistake more than once of over-thinking it and trying to over-explain to acquaintances, coworkers and family members to avoid the awkward pause in the conversation. Trust me when I say – if you don't want to explain more than "I decided to stop drinking" or my personal favorites, "alcohol makes me feel like crap", or a simple "no, thanks" when offered, then don't. That should be plenty. We will be referring to these statements as boundary phrases throughout the rest of the book.

It is *extremely* important to keep in mind that the only thing that is truly in our control is how we react to situations. We can not control the way other people behave. Once we accept this and put all of our efforts into improving our own attitudes, things start to come into focus. This is such a short, simple paragraph yet I wish I could highlight it or bookmark it for you. It is the basis of the serenity prayer.

...Grant me the serenity to accept the things I can not change
The courage to change the things I can
And the wisdom to know the difference

What I am going to say first is often a hard tactic for people to adopt. It was for me too, but I eventually realized it was something I needed to do. It is very possible that you will need to do this too. I found that I had to avoid, as much as I possibly could, any event where alcohol may be present until I was certain that I had my last craving that made me want to climb the walls of my apartment while simultaneously crawling out of my skin. If I put myself in these kinds of situations before I had gathered enough tools to handle it, I found my guard was down, whether I was keenly aware of it or not. It felt like it was going to be such a long time and that I was going to miss out on so many important things, but as I mentioned, I had my last true craving at four and a half months sober. In the scheme of things, it was a blip on my life's radar, and a very important time for me to focus on myself and find success in staying sober. I traded those boozy gatherings for trying new hobbies or attending sober events, as we discussed in Chapter 3. Once I felt strong enough, I started to make appearances at events with alcohol with my tools to stay sober in tow. At that point, I found them to be somewhat boring anyway, especially when people were becoming quite obviously intoxicated and weren't really "there" in our conversations anymore. If you choose to do this (and I recommend it), when you are invited to such an event during this time a simple "I'm busy that day, but I hope to see you soon!" will do the trick just fine.

Now, let's go over what it can look like to tell the different people in your life about your choice. Talking to friends, family, neighbors, and coworkers, can feel like navigating a minefield. I never knew how the conversation was going to go and that in itself made me anxious; especially when each group brings its own set of expectations, judgments, and, unfortunately, potential for disappointment. I soon learned the first step in managing these situations is identifying the triggers they might set off. Let's break it down:

Family and Friends:

With those closest to you, the fear of judgment can feel inescapable. People are much more willing to show you how they really feel, whether it be through words or body language. You might worry they'll view your choice as a challenge about their own drinking habits (like Kasey), or perhaps you're concerned they'll reminisce about the "good old days" when you'd join them in a drink, making you feel excluded or nostalgic for a life you're trying to leave behind. **Remember, while you cannot control their reactions, you can control your environment and the information you share.** Be prepared for questions but also know that you're not obligated to provide more detail than you're comfortable with. As I mentioned above, it's totally okay to say something like, "I'm not drinking because it's better for my health and happiness," and leave it at that.

Neighbors:

Neighbors can often be acquaintances we see frequently, but might not have deep relationships with. This dynamic can make it awkward to explain why you're suddenly turning down the wine at the neighborhood barbecue, especially when people are so used to seeing you bring an entire bottle, literally with your name on it, and polishing it off before the burgers are ready. In these cases, it's helpful to have a simple, polite decline ready to go, such as, "I'm taking a break from drinking, but I'd love a soda if you have one!" Almost always, they won't think anything of it, they'll be glad to see you doing well, and will respond with "Coke or Dr. Pepper?"

Coworkers:

The workplace can be one of the trickiest environments to navigate. From happy hours to holiday parties, alcohol often plays a central role in socializing. Anticipate these events and plan your responses. If possible, suggest activities that don't center around drinking. When drinking is involved, arm yourself with a response that feels authentic to you. Perhaps, "I've found I'm more productive and happier when I skip the alcohol," or simply, "I'm not drinking tonight, you all have fun!"

Staying True to Ourselves and Our Boundaries

It's important to recognize it's happening, respond constructively, and regroup when faced with a potential trigger. One very important way to do this is to stick to our guns when it comes to our boundaries. As women, we often feel guilty for setting boundaries. We are made to feel like we are supposed to sacrifice our own health and happiness to please those around us. For me, my boundaries with others were blurry at best, and it took a lot of practice to bring them into focus. It was a moment of clarity when I realized I shouldn't attend any event where there was going to be alcohol when I was still feeling fragile, so I set that boundary and it was a big part of my success in staying sober, as I mentioned it could be for you.

Or like when I told Kasey, I could have simply said "I'm not drinking because I feel better when I don't," without feeling like I had to explain myself more, knowing that I can share as much or as little as I damn well please about my choices. We can use positive visualization and scenario role-play to be more mentally prepared to stand strong when our sobriety, or even simply the *choice* to stay sober, is threatened.

Let's Talk Practical Application

Here are some ways to communicate your boundaries (with compassion) effectively and efficiently.

Ways to Communicate Your Boundaries:

- **Be Confident:** Your decision to stop drinking and your journey to staying sober are somethings you should be proud of. You're not "full of yourself" to want to carry this confidence in your conversations – matter of fact, you deserve to feel proud of this huge, personal milestone in your life. You also don't owe anyone an explanation, but if you choose to share, do so with confidence.

- **Practice Compassion If Possible:** Many people's reactions are more about themselves than they are about you. If you can remember this during the times of awkward silence or when someone says an off-putting passive aggressive comment, you'll be better off for it. If you have the energy, be ready to offer compassion both to yourself and to them, understanding that this might be challenging for them to understand or accept. However, if the conversation goes sour, always, and I mean *always*, go back to the confidence tip and confidently and kindly excuse yourself from the conversation. Your job right now is to work on you, not them.

- **Seek Support:** Before you start telling others, ensure you have a support system in place. This could be a therapist, a sober friend, or an online support group. They can offer advice, empathy, and encouragement when you need it most. They can also be great people to bring with you to events where alcohol is being served. Remember that it's better to walk away from a triggering situation instead of trying to appease others – your needs come first! ESPECIALLY now while you are protecting your sobriety as if it were a sweet, tender little baby that needs all of your attention.

Key Takeaways:

Articulate Your Boundaries, Clearly: Be compassionate yet straightforward when communicating your decision to not drink. Don't feel guilty over choosing what's best for you and keep it simple.

Have an Alternative Handy: When faced with a situation or environment where you're tempted to drink, have a non-alcoholic beverage always on hand. If you're with a friend, tell them about your situation and ask them to help keep things in check with you.

Preemptively Communicate to Family and Friends: Before heading to social situations or family gatherings where you may be offered or tempted to drink, tell your family and friends beforehand that you're choosing to remain sober and kindly ask them to respect your choice. If you have a bad feeling about going, just let them know you can't make it and that you hope to see them soon.

Your Well Being Comes First: Let go of personal guilt and shame that might be associated with peer pressure. Remember you don't need to over explain yourself and can simply say "I feel better when I don't drink."

Celebrate Each Small Victory: If you've just successfully managed one of your triggers, gotten through an especially difficult family gathering or have hit any other type of milestone, that's means to celebrate (in a way that doesn't cause you to relapse)! It is such a huge accomplishment every single time it happens.

Action Items:

Role-Playing Scenarios

Ask a supportive friend or someone in a recovery group to role-play various scenarios where you might be offered a drink by coworkers, friends, or family. Practice responding with the phrases suggested in this chapter, or a version of them that you feel good about. This exercise helps build confidence in declining drinks and explaining your sobriety in a supportive, low-pressure environment. It can also prepare you for unexpected reactions and teach you how to maintain your composure.

Journaling Your Triggers

Keep a journal for a week, noting every time you feel a trigger or a craving for alcohol. Next to each entry, write down what you think caused it and how you responded or could respond in the future. This exercise is designed to increase self-awareness about what situations or emotions prompt cravings and to develop personalized strategies for managing these triggers and how you react to them.

Crafting Your Script

Write down your own personalized scripts for declining alcohol in various social situations. Tailor your responses to reflect your personality, making sure they feel authentic to you. I can be a somewhat blunt person, so perhaps you want phrases that feel gentler. Then, practice these scripts out loud in front of a mirror. This exercise will help make you more comfortable and confident when explaining your sobriety to others.

Boundary Setting Workshop

Attend a workshop on setting healthy boundaries that is for people in addiction recovery. The workshop could cover how to communicate your needs respectfully and effectively, how to deal with pushback, and how to maintain your boundaries without feeling guilty. This educational setting provides tools and strategies for protecting your sobriety in social settings.

Support Circle Meetings

Join a support group meeting with others who are also in recovery. Use this time to discuss experiences, challenges, and successes in telling people about your decision to stop drinking. Share strategies that worked, explore feelings around being sober in a drinking world, and offer mutual support. This exercise fosters a sense of community and understanding, showing that you're not alone in your journey.

In the Next Chapter:

In the next chapter we'll talk about how we can think through the consequences of drinking and make better choices instead of falling back into old habits, allowing us to take back our own personal power.

Triggers Worksheet

Triggers are anything that brings back thoughts, feelings, or memories of an addiction. That is why triggers lead to cravings, and cravings can lead to relapse if we don't have the right tools in place to handle them.

Write down your triggers below as they happen. I've provided my own personal example to get you started. Note when they occur, why they occur and how you think you can respond to them so that you aren't at risk of relapse.

EXAMPLE:

Trigger:

I was invited to my best friend's "Bowling and Beer" birthday party.

How did this make you feel? Did it make you want to drink or use drugs or have a feeling that leads up to making you want to drink or use drugs?

It made me feel like I had no idea how I was going to resist the urge to have several pints of beer if I went. It definitely made me feel like I might drink if I went.

How did you or could you react? Could you have handled it better? Do you need to take a break from this person, place or thing?

I decided that it was time to tell my friend about my decision and that I couldn't go. I made sure to find something else to do so I was distracted during the time of the party (went to see a movie). Luckily, she was understanding and didn't make it about her. I stayed sober, she had a great time at her birthday party, and we have plans to get pedicures next week!

YOUR TURN:

Trigger:

_____

_____

How did this make you feel? Did it make you want to drink or use drugs or have a feeling that leads up to making you want to drink or use drugs?

_____

_____

_____

_____

_____

How did you react? Could you have handled it better? Do you need to take a break from this person, place or thing?

_____

_____

_____

_____

_____

_____

_____

Trigger:

_____

_____

How did this make you feel? Did it make you want to drink or use drugs or have a feeling that leads up to making you want to drink or use drugs?

_____

_____

_____

_____

_____

_____

How did you react? Could you have handled it better? Do you need to take a break from this person, place or thing?

_____

_____

_____

_____

_____

_____

_____

_____

_____

Trigger:

_____

_____

How did this make you feel? Did it make you want to drink or use drugs or have a feeling that leads up to making you want to drink or use drugs?

_____

_____

_____

_____

_____

_____

How did you react? Could you have handled it better? Do you need to take a break from this person, place or thing?

_____

_____

_____

_____

_____

_____

_____

_____

Trigger:

_____

_____

How did this make you feel? Did it make you want to drink or use drugs or have a feeling that leads up to making you want to drink or use drugs?

_____

_____

_____

_____

_____

_____

How did you react? Could you have handled it better? Do you need to take a break from this person, place or thing?

_____

_____

_____

_____

_____

_____

_____

_____

Now take this to your own notebook and keep going.

Think It Through

YOU MAY HAVE TO FIGHT A BATTLE MORE THAN ONCE TO WIN IT.

-MARGARET THATCHER

The Tape

In this chapter I'll break down what it looks like when you're faced with the decision to drink or use, and the strategies you can use to consistently say "no" to drinking or using.

Picture this: you're at a party, one where you didn't think there'd be much booze around to be an issue, but here you are, in the host's kitchen, all alone with the bottles of hard alcohol and the cooler of beer and there's this tiny little voice in your head. It's whispering to you, practically showing you the golden brick road towards that glittering, oh-so-tempting glass of *insert your drink of choice*... you start romanticizing about how good that first drink feels, the warm sensation in your stomach... QUEUE THE RECORD SCRATCH. Here is exactly when you do a little something that is known in the sober community as – *playing the tape forward.*

The "What If" Game (Step 1: Visualize)

Playing the tape forward is kind of like having a crystal ball but instead of half-baked fortunes or winning lottery numbers, it shows you the real-deal consequences of taking that first sip. I think we both know it's not just about the hangover that's waiting for us the next day, but the shame, guilt and baggage (that we'll talk more about in Chapter 6) we feel when we make that slapdash decision to take a drink. The "What If" Game is all about peering into the future and anticipating the full weight of your actions. Picture it like this – you're a few weeks into being sober and you're thinking you can handle your first party. You're feeling good, chatting with old friends and feeling in-control. After a while, you spot your drink of choice in the hands of a friend headed your way. You talk to them for awhile, catching up about this and that when they finally ask you *hey I'm going to get another, want one?* The scene pauses and you start to play through both scenarios…

Scene 1:

You say "yes" and that friend comes back with your drink of choice. You rip off your sobriety like a bandaid, you don't think about what you're doing, you just let the glass reach your lips and your muscle memory takes over from there. You keep talking and one thing leads to another, they mention something about a promotion or a volleyball tournament but you're only half listening… Then another drink leads to *just one more* and soon you catch yourself stumbling home. You pass out on your couch with your shoes and makeup still on and the TV blaring. A half pint of Jameson on your coffee table waiting to greet you in the morning when you come to. You wake up the morning after with a killer headache and a *deep urge to drink again… and then you do.* Aaaaand end scene.

Scene 2:

You pause and smile as you put your hand up and say one of the boundary phrases you learned in Chapter 4 – "actually, I decided to stop drinking for my happiness and health." Your friend simply says "okay, cool." You guys keep talking and have a great conversation. You learn that they've just got a promotion at work and won championships in their work volleyball league. You're able to share a genuine moment with them further building your friendship with that person. Eventually you both part ways and you end up heading home. You take a shower, do your skincare routine, and get a restful night's sleep. You wake up the next day refreshed, proud, and grateful you were able to say no (and your face feeling plump and youthful). End scene. The First Step to Success:

Successful Visualization

Visualize both scenarios that you're currently being faced with. Walk through the details as if you were living in that moment. Do this with both scenarios – the one where you decide to drink and the one where you don't.

It's important to get really detailed and deep about the shitstorm that would ensue if you made the decision to say "yes". For me, I would have woken up two days later in my apartment, not quite sure what day it was and afraid to look at the history of my text messages, which would certainly be mortifying. The unbearable doom, shame and anxiety would set in again, and I'd almost certainly drink again to escape it. There I'd be, right back in the cycle of despair and misery I'd worked so hard to get away from.

It's equally important to get just as detailed and deep if you had made the decision to stay sober. For me, I felt so incredibly good and proud of myself every morning I woke up, remembered the night before and had that extra momentum to keep going because I felt great and had finally made a good memory as opposed to another bad choice I was ashamed of.

The Domino Effect (Step 2: Break Down the Situation)

Let's say that you say "yes" to that first drink. Just like that first domino getting tipped over, you watch the rest fall into place – one after another. Just like your decision to drink. Now imagine each subsequent domino is a consequence of pushing over the first one:

Domino #2:

Mentally checking out of the conversation and not actively listening because you're too enamored with the fact that you're *finally having a drink.*

Domino #3:

Having several more drinks after you finally say something you regret to a close friend – most likely someone who already knows you've decided to stop drinking and tries to stop you from drinking more.

Domino #4:

You end up passing out at the end of the night with your shoes still on, your hair greasy from a night out and end up with a nasty headache the morning after. You then think *well fuck it, why not?* – and have **another drink.**

See how quickly that happened? Just like dominos, once we tip the first one over, it's hard to stop the rest as they gain momentum. That being said, the next step in the three steps to success method is breaking down the situation.

Breakdown the Situation

Break down the situation into as many little "dominos" as you can. Break down your first decision to drink (or not drink), how the night plays out and everything in-between. The more detailed you can be in breaking down the situation, the better you can visualize and play out the scenario that most benefits you.

Thinking it Through: The Sunny Side of Sobriety

Don't think it's all doom and gloom – making a solid choice amidst temptation can help you trust yourself more which, in turn, helps you hone your intuition and decision making. So, let's take a walk on the sunny side of sobriety and break down all of the different benefits of **not** drinking or using:

Having More Clarity

Waking up clear-headed, remembering everything from the night before and maybe even *enjoying your morning and morning routine.* When we're clear-headed, we're able to make decisions that don't just benefit present you, but future you as well. When I first got sober, I realized that many of my looming to-do list tasks seemed a lot more manageable when I was able to clearly think through each step I needed to take in order to accomplish that task.

Making Healthier Choices

When our bodies aren't constantly in recovery mode from the last bender, we're able to catch up on sleep, prep healthier meals for ourselves and overall feel confident within ourselves and the choices we're making. Now don't get me wrong – you're not going to wake up one morning and just completely be a different person, wanting to only eat apple slices and salads all day. No. What I'm saying is that you can tip the scales by making it *easier for yourself* to eat healthier – like making refrigerator oatmeal before bed and waking up to a healthy breakfast with some honey and fruit that you bought at the store earlier that week. We'll talk more about pampering yourself in Chapter 7, but the key idea here is to realize taking care of yourself isn't a chore, it's a form of self love.

Building More Genuine Relationships

When we're *really* present within our relationships, it allows us to not only build upon existing relationships with friends, family and coworkers but also opens the door to make new, genuine connections with people. Since we're also taking better care of our bodies and overall health, it's also easier to stay engaged within the conversation, actively listen to whom we're talking to and recall tidbits about their lives. Thus, further strengthening the bond you share with that person, and reinforcing your sense of community (like we discussed in Chapter 3). I have made so many dear friends and genuine connections with people since I have gotten sober; people who are there for me and I can show up for when they need me as well.

All Of the Above = Confidence

One great, big takeaway from choosing to stay sober is the positive snowball effect we encounter because we're taking more responsibility for our lives. Like I mentioned above, this includes being able to think through your decisions more clearly, spend better quality time with friends, build connections and care for yourself in a way that promotes your inner well-being. These are all building blocks to get you to the next level – building your overall confidence and belief in yourself! Awesome, right?!

Thinking It Through: The Doom and Gloom

Alright, so we talked about the sunny side of sobriety but let's say you decide to go the other way. Instead of following the yellow brick road, you go off on just a short detour, a one-way ticket back to active addition. I know you might already be thinking about what that might look like but let's break it down anyway so this practice really sinks in:

The Pang of Regret

Although that first sip of alcohol might feel pretty good, regret is even better at lurking in the corner of your bad decisions and present mistakes. We've all felt that crushing feeling like a hand going straight into our chest cavity and pulling on our heart – followed by a thought along the lines of *what did I just do?* Whether it's an off-putting comment to a close friend or a full-on psychotic episode in a public place, more often than not, these regrettable moments aren't things we can fix with just an apology or countless cups of coffee and donuts….

Less Clarity and Unhealthy Choices

Yes, you guessed it. If you're back to drinking regularly you might be waking up with that throbbing headache and the urge to drink again. Not only to escape the headache but the overpowering feeling of regret as well. Coupled with the fact that if you're on a huge bender you'll be eating the quickest, most convenient food choices around, if any food at all.

Strained Relationships

Missed birthdays, half-hearted apologies and faith that's been chipped away with every broken promise – it's near impossible to maintain (not even cultivate, just maintain) the relationships you have and be a full-on alcoholic. Just like the domino effect, if you're drinking, you're not taking care of yourself and you're not able to take care of others, and if you're unable to do both those things, you're most likely not going to retain what's going on in a simple one-on-one conversation or interaction. Unlike the sunny side of sobriety, as time goes on, this chips away at your personal relationships with friends, family and coworkers – allowing your connection to them to slowly wither away until they give up hope entirely. I know this sounds harsh but like I said in the introduction, I'm going to tell it how it is and how bad it *could get*, if it is not like this already. **Remember, you always have the power to choose the life you want to live – that's *always* up to you.**

Less Confidence More Stalled Dreams

When we allow alcohol to be the key decision maker in our lives it also becomes our number one hobby, lifestyle goal and how we start to identify ourselves. The catch is that when we see ourselves as just "the partier" or "the fun uncle/aunt" or even "the fun friend", we start to embed that core belief into who we are. For example, we may start to tell ourselves other self-limiting beliefs that support our drinking habit like how drinking makes us more fun or how our friends wouldn't want to spend time with us if we're sober because we're boring.

When we're tackling our lives with a clear mind, it's much easier to stop ourselves from spinning this false narrative but when we're always hungover or buzzed, our lives seem to mesh together like smooshing together all the colors of a clay putty. Not only can we not see ourselves, our obstacles or our lives clearly but we also tend to lose respect for ourselves. Each time we decide to take a sip and let alcohol envelop our lives again, the little voice that tells us *you'll never get sober, you have no idea how to live without alcohol,* or worse, *you don't deserve to get sober, you're an awful human being,* gets louder and louder. The more we let our drinking continue, the louder and more awful that voice becomes.

Now that we've gone through both sides of the narrative, let's talk about what you can do to overcome the urge to drink when the opportunity arises and make a positive choice for your present and future self.

Do The Right Thing (Step 3: Make A Positive Choice)

After you break things down in step two, it's time to make a choice. More often than not, we think that we have to be brave or bold or sure of ourselves 100% of the time and that's how we'll be the superheroes of sobriety. Realistically, it's just that one moment – the moment where we're introduced to temptation where we can practice playing the tape all the way through and thinking to ourselves *I'm just going to do the right thing, right here, right now* and then we do. We say "no thank you, not right now."

Key Takeaways:

Steps To Success

1. Visualize both scenarios.
2. Breakdown the situation into as many little "dominos" as you can.
3. Make a positive choice for yourself.

Take Back Your Power: Remember, you always have the power to choose the life you want to live – that's always up to you. Don't be afraid to say "no" to situations, people or places that you feel might be triggering to you, especially in the early stages of your sobriety. You need to put yourself first in order to be the best version of you.

Practice Makes Things Easier: Although as humans we're seldomly perfect, practice does make it easier to say "no" when the opportunity to drink does arise. By using the three steps (visualize, break down the situation and make a positive choice) we can consistently make better choices for ourselves. There's also a variety of ways we can practice these steps independently, as I'll get into with the action items.

See the Sunny Side of Sobriety: There are so many benefits that come with being present in your own life, as I listed above. Don't hesitate to walk yourself through all of the things you can do better because you're taking responsibility for your life, like building quality relationships with friends, nurturing connections, making healthier decisions, etc.…

Action Items:

Now that you're equipped with the tools and steps to succeed, it's time to practice! There are many ways we can go about this and I find that a little bit of everything goes a long way. As you start to practice on your own, you'll find what best works for you. Here are some action items to get you started:

Visualization: Pop in some calming music and focus on a scenario in which you're offered a drink. Imagine the environment, yourself and the person as vividly as you can. Imagine how you feel when you're first offered your drink (or substance) or choice. Afterwards, visualize saying "no". Whether you exit the conversation, phone a friend, use a boundary phrase or simply walk away is up to you. The more ways you can imagine yourself playing the tape forward and then saying "no" during that crucial moment, the easier it becomes when you're faced with the real thing.

Positive Encouragement: Put your hands on your hips (or another alternative that feels both comfortable and powerful in stance) and shower yourself with words of encouragement. The more specific you can be the better. For instance, instead of saying *I can do it,* you could say *I know that at this dinner party tonight I am able to say "no" with confidence because I know what's best for me, my body and my health. I will not feel bad over taking control of my own life. I love and accept myself for who I am and love who I'm becoming.* Feel free to also brainstorm these affirmations in advance so you don't get stumped. Eventually speaking to yourself in a compassionate way will become second nature!

Celebrate Your Wins: Like I mentioned in previous chapters, it's important to document and celebrate your wins. When you do something you find special – like refuse your drink of choice or choose to use a boundary phrase that helps you live your best life – celebrate. Celebrate in a way that is unique to you, like having your favorite dessert, drawing yourself a bath, or buying yourself a small treat or item you've been wanting. Trust me, you're totally worth it and you should celebrate your mini-milestones.

Phone a Friend (Seek Support): I'm sure by now you've noticed that this is a constant action item throughout all of our chapters. This is because there is no hard and fast rule when it comes to seeking support during your journey through sobriety. Some days you might feel like you're on top of the world while others might leave you feeling like you just want to crawl into a corner of your room and never come out. It's always important to have a support system in place whether, it's a trusted friend that knows what's going on, your AA sponsor, addiction counselor or an online community. Remember, seeking community is an act of courage and compassion for yourself and those that love you.

In the Next Chapter

In the next chapter we'll talk about visualizing and unpacking the baggage of your past mistakes and regrets. By addressing each issue one at a time, we can lighten the burden of guilt and shame and move forward with clarity and purpose.

The Sobriety Ledger

In the exercise below, we'll create a list of benefits of sobriety and the consequences of drinking, then dive deeper into different scenarios for us to practice the first two steps discussed in this chapter. By taking that split second to (1) visualize and (2) breakdown the scenario we're better equipped to follow step (3) when the time comes – making a positive choice that will benefit our future selves.

Some of the benefits of sobriety for me personally include:

_____

_____

_____

_____

_____

_____

_____

_____

_____

Some consequences of drinking for me specifically include:

_____

_____

_____

_____

_____

_____

_____

_____

_____

Scenario 1: (Example)

I'm at a baseball game with an old friend who innocently forgot I've stopped drinking and they've just come back from the snack stand with two ice-cold cups of beer.

Visualize

They're wearing a SF Giants jersey and holding two clear cups of cold, foamy beer. It's a hot day and I'm sweating with my baseball cap on. My mouth starts watering as I see them heading back and I see their face smiling back at me. They finally get back to their seats and offer me the beer, I put my hand on their shoulder and tell them, *Actually, I don't drink anymore* just as the loudspeaker announces something. They look at me quizzically then shrug their shoulders and say *okay, no pressure, totally forgot*. I smile back at them and we enjoy the game.

Breakdown the Situation

First domino (positive outcome) – I choose to not accept the drink, we keep watching the game, the Giants score a home run, my friend and I celebrate and we take the train home, laughing and catching up on what's been going on in our lives. I get a good night's sleep and wake up smiling, because it was such a great day. Now I have a recent good memory to look back on instead of another bad night I wish never happened.

First domino (negative outcome) – I choose to accept the drink and it goes down so smooth I end up chugging the whole thing. My friend looks over at me and says *easy there, tiger, it's the first inning*. Fast forward to the 5th inning and I'm seven beers in, not even realizing they stopped at two. I'm getting really hazy on all the details and I hear people cheering, I think the Giants scored or got a touchdown because everyone starts going nuts. My friend glances over at me and we cheer. I throw up just before we get on the train heading home. The train ride home is rather silent and my friend scrolls on their phone.

Now try this for yourself using our scenarios and your visualization skills!

Scenario 2:

I'm at the county fair with my family and someone suggests we all should take shots.

Visualize

_____

_____

_____

_____

_____

_____

Breakdown the Situation

Positive Outcome:

_____

_____

_____

_____

_____

_____

Negative Outcome:

_____

_____

_____

_____

_____

Scenario 3:

I'm at a dinner party and the host suggests that we try the wine they brought back from Italy.

Visualize

_____
_____
_____
_____
_____
_____

Breakdown the Situation

Positive Outcome:

_____
_____
_____
_____
_____
_____

Negative Outcome:

_____
_____
_____
_____
_____

Scenario 4:

I'm on a date and they flag down the waiter and ask me, "What are you drinking tonight?"

Visualize

Breakdown the Situation

Positive Outcome:

Negative Outcome:

Scenario 5:

I'm consoling a dear friend who's going through a breakup. They start pouring themselves a vodka soda and turn to me to ask, "you want one?"

Visualize

_____

_____

_____

_____

_____

_____

Breakdown the Situation

Positive Outcome:

_____

_____

_____

_____

_____

_____

Negative Outcome:

_____

_____

_____

_____

_____

The Suitcase Method – Lightening Your Load

FORGIVENESS IS THE FRAGRANCE THAT THE VIOLET SHEDS ON THE HEEL THAT HAS CRUSHED IT.

-MARK TWAIN

What It Is

Picture this – you're going about your day-to-day life, dragging around this awful, torn at the corners, beaten and battered suitcase. You're tired of rolling it around with its plastic wheels, often getting caught on large cracks in pavement or tipping over at a moment's notice and pulling you down. Now imagine that this suitcase is filled with your past regrets, mistakes, what-if moments, ignored responsibilities and worst case scenarios. All of the things that have kept you drinking or using, because they were too painful to face, are shoved inside of this suitcase. Not only that, the suitcase becomes heavier and heavier as the pile of problems your addiction has caused, and continues to cause, grows. All of that gets stuffed into this suitcase as well. This suitcase is with you, always. Is this starting to sound familiar? Well, much like the rest of the population, you probably have baggage. How much baggage depends on you. The good news is that just as you start to get weighed down by your regrets and past mistakes, there is a way to unpack your suitcase so that you can spring forward into life feeling lighter and more at ease in the long-run. Now how do we do that, you ask? By facing and focusing on *one past debacle, demon or pile of wreckage at a time*. We can slowly unpack what needs to be unpacked and gently handle things with a mix of courage, compassion and self-forgiveness. This is something that I have always thought of as The Suitcase Method.

Open the Suitcase

You've been carrying this thing around for years, it keeps getting heavier and heavier, and it has been even longer since you have opened it to deal with what is inside, if you have ever opened it at all. Now close your eyes and imagine hoisting it onto your bed at home. You're fed up and sick of carrying this shit around with you everywhere you go and now that you have the tools to stop adding to the suitcase by continuing to drink or use, you feel the fight in you to face what is inside. You unzip it and flop it open. Just as you suspected, it is filled with a mix of painful memories, regrets, shameful moments, false steps, debts and every stumble in life you've ever taken. What is the first trauma, mistake or regret you see? Pull it out and set it aside.

Now, without hesitation, imagine yourself closing the suitcase, zipping it up and putting it deep in the back of your closet. Store it there for now. You won't be carrying the rest of the suitcase with you everywhere you go anymore. Every time you think of all of these bad things all at once, just imagine shoving them back into that suitcase at the back of your closet, not to be forgotten about, but to be handled when you are ready. Your job right now is to focus on whatever it is you took out and set aside. We are going to focus on coming to terms with that one thing until you feel good about it. Once you do, imagine yourself repeating the process with the suitcase. Drag it out of the closet, open it up, take one thing out, then put the suitcase right back in your closet. Repeat this process until it is empty. Then always remember to check on the suitcase from time to time, so that it doesn't get too heavy again.

Remember the to-dos and the done list we talked about in Chapter 1? And then we talked about leveling up on your list of to-dos. We are about to level up big time by taking care of our suitcase that is splitting at the seams with to-dos, and we aren't talking about washing our hair.

Please note: The FIRST thing we need to take out of the suitcase is our addiction, and learning the tools to not drink or use.

Lightening Your Load – Step by Step

One of the first things I pulled out of my suitcase was my $18,000 credit card debt that I had acquired. I had no clue how I was going to handle it but I carried that problem, and only that problem, with me for about a week, until one day I was wandering aimlessly around our downtown area and saw a bank. Without thinking anything about what I was going to do or say, I went inside. "Good morning, what can we help you with today?" a man in a suit asked. "I need help with my credit card debt," I said bluntly. I figured he would see me to the door right then and there (I didn't even have an account at this bank), but he smiled and took me to his desk and invited me to have a seat.

In no time I was learning about the wonderful world of 0% APR credit cards, balance transfers and tracking my credit score. I had a plan in place to pay down my debt in a matter of 30 minutes (and made it happen in two years and one month). Shortly after I had this encounter in the bank and felt good about my payment plan, I got that suitcase back out and pulled out the next thing that I needed to face.

I want to point out that I never would have been able to handle this had I not asked for help. Asking for help is something I was terrible at, yet it is so critical to being able to navigate this world, and to our survival.

Recognition – Facing Our Past Head On

Imagine what you took out of the suitcase was an old photograph of you and someone important to you that has been hurt by your behavior. You carry it with you in your pocket, the suitcase tucked away, your closet holding your overall burden for you without you having to carry it around all of the time. You take your time to fully look at the photograph, allowing yourself to get lost in and process the emotions of that relationship. Much like our memories, some photos allow you to get lost in happy and warm moments, while others remind you of instances you'd much rather forget. It's important to take a good look at what happened and get brutally honest with yourself about it. Take a deep breath, close your eyes, and say out loud to yourself "I forgive me. I was not myself when this happened." Try it now. Feels good, right? Do this often and in general.

We will talk more about the chemical hijack of addiction in Chapter 10 and how it alters our brains in such a way where we do things that are literally outside of our control when we are in active addiction. Understanding the science behind this will aid in your ability to forgive yourself for your actions while you were chained down by your addiction.

Get Practical

Now that we have felt the feelings and gotten honest with ourselves about what happened, it is time to get practical. What can we do to fix it? Least of all, we owe that person an apology, but we have to gauge the situation. How hurt are they? Do they refuse to speak to us? Do they need space? Are they still in our lives, but consistently make cutting remarks about our character? Depending on the person, we will need to handle it accordingly. In many instances, a heartfelt letter is most appropriate where we take full responsibility for our actions and how we hurt them. Do not say anything about their behavior (even though they may have hurt you, too, somehow). Just own up to yours. Send it off and give them as much time as they need to process it and continue to tell yourself that you forgive you, and you were not yourself when you hurt them. On to the next piece of balled-up wreckage in your suitcase...

To sum it up, the process looks like this: 1.) pick one and only one issue to face at a time 2.) take a good hard look at it, feel the feelings, and then get brutally honest with yourself about the situation you are facing 3.) come up with a practical solution to handle it 4.) don't move on to the next thing until you feel good about the plan of action for the one at hand, and 5.) YOU WILL VERY LIKELY NEED TO ASK FOR HELP TO FIGURE IT OUT. I had help from my supportive community.

Self Love – Forgiving Ourselves

When we look at what we could learn from ourselves in those past moments, we open up to the idea of forgiving ourselves for our faults. This can happen in several ways, but in my experience these were the most profound realizations I had that helped me forgive myself:

1. We either let go by realizing we did the best we could in that moment with the tools we were given at the time.

2. We learn to love ourselves more now so that we can look back at our past selves with the same compassion we would give to a sick friend (not an easy task, but it can be accomplished by putting into practice the techniques outlined in this book).

3. The more we practice forgiving others for their wrongdoings (also not easy… but we are nowhere near perfect either), the easier it becomes to forgive ourselves for our own.

By acknowledging that you messed up *but also learned and grew from that moment,* you make room for yourself to move on and shed that extra baggage.

Here We Go With Gratitude Again…

Now it's time to find the silver linings! It's time to sift through each less-than-graceful memory you're working to forgive yourself for and think about how you can find gratitude within each less-than-desirable situation. Let's use an example – one of my shining moments was falling asleep on the floor at a party at my friend's house, with no recollection of the night's activities or how I even got to my friend's house. I woke up with one shoe missing, some broken sunglasses and a bloody lip. I got yet another talking to from another friend about how I needed help; but this time was different. Something actually sank in and it was then I realized I had a drinking problem and that it was *actually* negatively affecting my life. I didn't say so out loud, but I definitely admitted it internally. If you were to ask me to find gratitude in that moment while I was living it, I may have had some choice words in return, but I'm grateful for that moment and especially grateful for that friend for not sending me packing.

After all, if I hadn't had that moment of clarity, I might not have realized I needed help, I might not have gotten sober and had my sons whom I am absolutely obsessed with, and I might not have been able to fulfill my childhood dream of writing a book (even though this isn't *exactly* what I had imagined!), but here we are.

The real difficulty is to overcome how you think about yourself.
– Maya Angelou

Don't Forget Your *BONUSES*

Don't forget to scan the QR code or visit this link: www.myhappysoberlife.com so you can download your bonus gratitude journal. Also included: a guide on getting out of a bad living situation and a guide on getting good sleep.

The Science Behind the Suitcase Method

Although this specific visualization technique and the term "The Suitcase Method" is something I came up with on my own, I was surprised to learn that visualizing a container for all of your problems that you will keep somewhere safe is actually a tried-and-true practice that is actively used in therapy to help people cope with past traumas.

It can be incredibly powerful to help with self-forgiveness and reflecting on your past wrongdoings as well. Research explains that reflection and self-forgiveness practices can positively affect our mental well-being, acting as an emotional "detox," clearing out psychological clutter so we can make way for positive growth and new beginnings.

An important practice to help move through these issues is writing, or journaling. Studies such as those conducted by Lee, Gerhart, Braynen, and Bonifas (2019) have shown that engaging in reflective writing exercises can also have a positive impact on brain health, promoting a sense of well-being and reducing stress. Their research emphasizes the beneficial effects of writing about one's experiences, thoughts, and feelings, which can lead to a heightened state of mental clarity and emotional relief – AKA unpacking and letting go of our psychological baggage. At the end of this chapter, we'll use the "Letter to Myself" exercise to start building our self-forgiveness muscle memory.

The work of Bos, Kuiper, and Van Raalten (2018) reinforces this idea by highlighting how our brains respond to habit forming processes like self-forgiveness. When we continuously practice the act of forgiveness, we strengthen our muscle memory and the neural pathways associated with positive self-reflection. This can help us foster long-term mental resilience, promote positive self talk and emotionally recover from past traumatic experiences.

Key Takeaways

Unpack, Don't Discard: Unpacking our past isn't about throwing away our history or letting bad memories rot in the corner of our minds only to drag us down time and time again. It's about owning up to the messes we made, creating space for new experiences, learning from our past mistakes and letting ourselves step into a lighter, less bogged down future.

Lessons and Silver Linings: When looking through old memories, especially the most painful ones, try to find the lesson and the silver lining those experiences provided you. How did those past regrets or mistakes allow you to be who you are today? Bring gratitude and logic to your past memories so you can rectify what happened as much as possible, and better manage a similar situation in the future.

Look Ahead:

With our suitcases feeling light and our hearts at ease, we're able to look to the future without dragging our past with us. Although this doesn't mean that we'll never make another mistake in the future, we can make space for new experiences, adventures and find joy in the next chapter of our lives.

Action Items

Schedule Your Suitcase Session: Sit down and close your eyes and visualize taking your first thing out of your suitcase. Make sure to be free of any other distractions so you can truly focus and get honest with yourself about what happened, and come up with a solution that feels good to you. Don't forget to consider how you can ask for help each and every time. This can be as simple as feedback from a trusted friend.

Letter to Yourself: Write a letter to your past self, acknowledging the mistakes you've made and expressing forgiveness and acceptance. Try to be your most authentic and vulnerable self in this letter, knowing that it's for you and only you to read. Be open and honest with yourself and forgive yourself for your past wrongdoings and mistakes. End the letter with a kind and compassionate word of encouragement to yourself.

In the Next Chapter

In the next chapter, we'll indulge in self-care activities that bring you comfort and pleasure without compromising your sobriety. Let's learn to treat ourselves to guilt-free indulgences as a healthy alternative to alcohol and other negative substances.

A Letter To Myself

When you write your letter to your past self, be honest about your prior mistakes and take ownership of them. Acknowledge your past errors and failings and accept full responsibility for them. Emphasize forgiveness, but don't make excuses. Accept what you have done, forgive yourself for it, and remind yourself of the lessons you learned from this incident. As you conclude your letter, offer some kind, compassionate words of encouragement that will allow you to move forward from this and signal your intention to be better in the future. If you find this part difficult, it may help to imagine you are consoling a friend instead of yourself as you write it, and then when you read it again, switch it back to you. Get some tissues... I think you might need them :)

_____

_____

_____

_____

_____

_____

_____

_____

_____

_____

_____

_____

_____

_____

_____

_____

_____

_____

_____

_____

_____

_____

_____

_____

_____

_____

_____

_____

_____

_____

_____

_____

_____

_____

_____

_____

_____

_____

_____

_____

_____

_____

_____

_____

_____

I forgive you, and I love you,

x_____

References:

Bos, D. J., Kuiper, R. M., & Van Raalten, T. R. (2018). Understanding the role of the ventromedial prefrontal cortex in memory encoding across the lifespan. *The Journal of Neuroscience*, 38(44), 9389-9391.

Lee, S. W., Gerhart, J., Braynen, T., & Bonifas, R. P. (2019). The effects of reflective writing exercises on the brain health of pregnant women. *Journal of Clinical Medicine*, 8(4), 451.

Permission to Splurge Otherwise

SELF-CARE IS HOW YOU TAKE YOUR POWER BACK.

–LALAH DELIA

The New You

It's 5pm on Saturday night. The past you might have already been drunk off of thermos wine at your daughter's soccer game around this time, or been pregaming at a friend's place before going out for a night on the town. Since you've been sober, you've been avoiding places that might be triggering like bars, PTA meetings or your ex-boyfriend's bed, so now you're not quite sure what to do with yourself. Now THIS is where the magic happens – where you're able to shower yourself with positive guilt-free indulgences, also known as self-care.

Self Indulgence vs Self-Care

Let's say there are two different types of self-care in the forms of our best friends, like two angels on either shoulder. There's *self indulgence,* whose wings are sparkling with diamonds. She's dressed to the nines in her finest gown, gently perched on your shoulder telling you that *you deserve that pair of $2,000 Jimmy Choos*. Self indulgence isn't only about living your best life but *indulging* in the finer things in life, in the luxuries we want but don't often let ourselves have.

Now let's look at the other shoulder – here we have *self-care*. She's a bit more laid back, has on a nice top and some comfy jeans. Unlike her sister, she's more down to earth, she loves caring for herself in all of the everyday, "the little things" types of ways. Self-care is the type of friend that loves having you come over and bakes homemade muffins, makes you tea and reminds you that you're really something special.

Caring for yourself is not self-indulgence, it is self-preservation, and that is an act of political warfare.

– Audre Lorde

Rich Like Truffles and Fine Chocolate

I think it's clear that self indulgence and self-care are in the same ballpark but definitely aren't the same player and that's okay. There's a time and place for both – just in different frequencies. If self indulgence was a food, it'd be something incredibly *rich, chocolatey, almost velvet* on your tongue. Like most people, I love food like this but can only have so much and only every so often. *This is what self indulgence feels like.* It's a wonderful thing to treat yourself to that new iPad or a trip to the spa but if not done sparingly, these things can lead to *over-indulgence* which can negatively impact our lives almost as much as alcohol (or drug) abuse did. My point being that there are levels to splurging and if done thoughtfully, it can be a great way to reward yourself for overcoming a milestone; but splurging everyday isn't an act of self-love, it's a lack of self-control, paired with a different kind of rush – one that those who've suffered from drug addiction are all too familiar with...

Please note: if you are feeling desperate to get through a craving that feels like it has you by the throat, and the *only* thing that seems like it will help get you through it is an entire bag of spicy nacho Doritos, then by all means, go to town on that bag of Doritos and queue up some shows on Netflix. It is much better than the alternative of giving in and getting plastered. I had my fair share of moments like this in my first five months or so. My husband and I got sober together; he used to scout the candy aisle of Walgreens and buy whatever bags of chocolate were on sale and stay up late watching "Dexter". Once you feel steady on your sober feet, you'll want to make sure to move on from this, of course… and do try to use other tools to get you through it before you use this tactic. It's kind of like the tool at the back of your shed that's broken, you should and will get rid of it, but it still does the job well enough… for now.

The Expensive A** Earmuffs

It was the first winter I was sober and I went up with my friends to Lake Tahoe (a popular Northern California spot for skiing) where one of my high school friends owned a cabin. I was so excited to go as my parents had often taken me skiing there as a child. I could already smell the fresh, cold mountain air filling my nostrils. I'd also had a rather stressful week at work so this little long-weekend getaway came at the perfect time. We had just gotten up to the ski resort and we were on our first run of the day. I was sitting with two other friends on the lift and wanted to snap a selfie of us all. Naturally, we hit a bump at the exact wrong moment and although I managed to save my phone from certain death by chairlift, I wasn't able to save my beloved (yet worn) earmuffs.

I was at one of the most expensive ski resorts in the area. My friends and I had all splurged on a big resort since we didn't have to worry about getting a hotel and it was only a few days. Since I got sober around 8 months ago and had started my credit card repayment plan, I finally felt like I was on solid ground financially and I was proud of myself for that.

Now back to the earmuffs. My ears were freezing and I mean cherry red, I-can't-feel-anything type of frozen. After three runs, I'd had enough and lugged myself and my chunky ski boots into the nearest store. I made my way past the counter of goggles, new snow jackets, jumpers and headed towards the earmuffs. I saw the most lovely pair of fluffy, cream colored earmuffs. I checked the price tag and almost choked. *That much for EARMUFFS?!* I thought to myself as I ran the soft fabric through my fingers. *You know what, I deserve it.* I thought to myself, and with that I bought the earmuffs and enjoyed a great day on the slopes with my friends.

The moral of the story being I made a logical, healthy choice to indulge on something I wanted and happened to need, in a healthy and manageable way. Now if I had let's say, bought the earmuffs, a coat I didn't need, then hit the slots on the way back home – that'd be a different story entirely…

Self-Care Is Everyday

Unlike self indulgence, self-care is like the everyday angel. Self-care done consistently, shows like little happy sparkles in your life, reminding you how much you deserve to be loved and cared for by you. Much like the metaphor of self-indulgence being a rich chocolate, self-care is like that healthy gourmet dinner. It's warm and welcoming, like a nice long hug with a childhood friend or a perfect beach day. Self-care is something that you feel capable of doing daily, and it makes you feel good each and every time. There is never a feeling of guilt with self-care, like there can be with self indulgence (e.g. getting carried away and eating the whole freaking bag of chocolates vs. oops, I ate too many roasted brussel sprouts with balsamic reduction, truffle oil and sea salt).

You yourself, as much as anybody in the entire universe, deserve your love and affection.
– Buddha

You, yes, you, deserve all of your own affection, care, love and attention. Like we covered in Chapter 6 – it doesn't matter what you've done in the past. You've already let go of that baggage and nothing, (yes, I said *nothing*) can make you undeserving of self-love. Think of the worst thing you've ever done to someone. It can be anything from punching your best friend on the playground to getting back together with that toxic ex after you explicitly told your friends and family you wouldn't do that. Take it all in, feel it and now tell yourself – *nothing I could ever do or will do will make me any less deserving of love.* Rinse and repeat as necessary.

In all seriousness, loving ourselves is not only an act of service to us but to those around us. Just like the domino effect in Chapter 5, the first domino leads to the next leads to the next and so on and so forth. Let's play one of my self-care stories as an example.

The Store Run

It had been an especially stressful week at work and I was feeling overwhelmed to say the least. I had just finished work around 7pm and I was exhausted. All I wanted was to hop in my car, go to the nearest taqueria, order a super burrito and call it a day… BUT, I knew I didn't have any food at home, so instead, I hopped in my car, turned on my favorite podcast and headed to the local supermarket like a good girl. As I wandered zombie-like through the aisles I saw the "This Just In!" sign and I thought to myself *I deserve a treat.* I chose a lavender bath bomb and aloe vera face mask. For dinner, I decided to go French and fancy. I picked out some fig and brie cheese, prosciutto (Italian), a baguette and a small pack of chocolate madeleines. I finished up my shopping and headed home. I ate my dinner while watching some old "Friends" episodes and ended my day with a hot bath and face mask. I was sleepy, but happy and cared for, by me.

Although it took much more energy to get myself to the store, do my grocery shopping and still draw myself a bath at the end of the day – it was much more rewarding to care for myself well, *to love myself enough to make the effort*, than it would have if I had just done the easy thing and gone to the taqueria and woken up with burrito bloat, without having bathed or bought food for the next day.

Indulge in your own self-care like it's your ritual of love to yourself.

– Nitika Chopra

The Self-care Guilt

In a world where someone, somewhere, needs something from us, all the time – it can be difficult to not only make time for yourself but *allow yourself* to put your needs before others. In one way or another, the general public got the idea that caring for ourselves was selfish and even irresponsible (like calling in a mental health day from work or cutting someone out of our lives who has been dragging us down) – crazy, right? Indulging in a little me-time or putting yourself and your self-care routine first doesn't make you selfish, *it allows you to better care for yourself and thus, those that you love as well.* Caring for yourself is the ultimate act of self love – but how do we know that we're actually practicing self-care?

The Friend Theory

The friend theory goes like this – if you wouldn't treat your good friend the way you're treating yourself, you probably should make a few adjustments. For instance, one of my best friends from high school had a really important interview coming up just after we graduated college. Around a week before she got the most awful, heinous, can't get out of bed type, food poisoning. She was devastated. She called me crying, telling me how this was her dream job, how she couldn't reschedule the interview and how she was full-on freaking out. After I managed to calm her down, I packed a few things in my bag, stopped by the store for some chicken soup, Tums and a whole lot of peppermint tea and went off to her house. I worked a few minutes from her place and spent the week at hers helping her heal up, doing a bit of laundry for her and by the end of the week, she was well enough to make her interview. I remember she came back from the interview grinning from ear to ear. She screamed "I got the job! They hired me on the spot!!" We jumped up and down, hugged and I told her they'd be crazy if they hadn't. She still works for *National Geographic* – now in a much more high profile role but I like to think back to the day of her interview, and it makes me feel good to know I may have played a part in her success.

Now let's flip the script – let's say I got food poisoning, how would I treat *myself?* Sadly, most of us treat our friends and family much better than we treat ourselves, especially when it comes to positive self talk and overall commitment to self-care. If it were me, I wouldn't have called anyone, I would have tried to muscle through, tried to do the interview, and most likely would have botched it and be forced to take a week off because I'd overworked myself. I realize as I write this that something similar *did* happen to me… in sobriety! My youngest son had to go to the NICU after he was born and needed three surgeries. I had applied for a job before he was born and the interview was scheduled when he was two weeks old. I was a mess, but I didn't do anything to help myself be well for the interview, and I BOMBED it. I could have played that much differently! All in all, I didn't care about anything at that time but my son getting well, so I was fine with it and felt I should have just withdrawn my candidacy anyway.

I'm sure you can relate to a few similar circumstances where you've tried to push through when you really should have just taken care of yourself. I still have to be very careful not to do this.

Entering a Guilt-Free Zone

Remember in the last chapter how we talk about forgiving ourselves so we can let go of our baggage? Well very similarly, we've got to let go of our self-care guilt and put ourselves first. If that friend or family member deserves your love, attention and care, what makes you think that you don't deserve the same? You totally deserve it. Like I talked about above, caring for yourself doesn't mean constant extravagant spending benders or ignoring your daily responsibilities. It's acknowledging that you are a magnificent work in progress and you're worth the extra effort it takes to make your life a beautiful and enjoyable existence.

A study by Kim et. al. (2021) dove deep into what it means to practice self-care both for ourselves and how it positively affects our world. The study revealed that when we use self-care practices on a daily and weekly basis to the point where it's integrated in our lives, we're more capable of overcoming obstacles in our lives and more capable of caring for those we love.

The study specifically followed caregiving specialists who were told to practice self-care in several different forms on a daily basis. After some time, the researchers discovered that not only were the caregivers happier and more content with their own health and happiness, but that they were also more equipped to serve others more efficiently.

So, the next time you feel guilty over taking some "me-time," remember that you're not just doing this for yourself but for the ones you love as well.

DIY Your Routine

The more you personalize your self-care routine the more enjoyable it can be for you. We'll get you started with some foundational building blocks in the worksheet below but as you start to practice self-care, try making small changes and tweaks to make it fit what feels most fulfilling to you.

For example, I love skin care, but there are so many ways that can be done: retinol, oil and moisturizer; a Korean 10 step routine; a gel mask and a gua sha, to name a few. You may prefer a five mile run, but would you rather do it in a gym on a treadmill, through your neighborhood, or along a trail? If you need to process your feelings, do you prefer a good shower cry, a guided meditation, or going to the batting cages so you can let off steam by hitting some balls (I like all of these!)? Be thoughtful about what you do for yourself and *how* you do it, because the more you listen to your intuition about what is most soothing to you, the more at peace and content your self-care routine will make you feel. So do it the way YOU want to do it, gosh darn it!

Key Takeaways:

Self-care Is Essential: Putting in the extra effort for yourself on a day-to-day basis is a non-negotiable and healthy way to practice self love. It's also a vital part of maintaining sobriety because a clear mind and healthy body allows you to make better choices for yourself and those around you.

Leave the Guilt at the Door: It's not selfish to take care of yourself. Actually, it's not only for yourself but for those around you that you love. When you're able to take good care of yourself, you're able to better care for others.

Self Indulgence Isn't Self-care: Although self indulgence and self-care are in the same ballpark, one is much more day-to-day versus indulging in something you really want but don't quite need. Remember to practice healthy boundaries with yourself by practicing self-care daily, not extravagant, unhealthy and expensive acts of self indulgence, daily.

Personalize Your Routine: When we make our routine personalized to us, we can really enjoy putting the time and effort into creating a beautiful life for ourselves.

Action Items:

The Self-care Jar: Choose an activity that you can do each week that requires more time than your average day-to-day self-care routine like attending a new yoga class, exploring a new hobby or cooking a special Friday after-work meal for yourself. Write about how you'll schedule this new activity into your weekly plans.

Self-care vs Self Indulgence: Write 10 instances of self-care versus self indulgence. Remember that self indulgence is something that happens once in a while versus how self-care is a daily action item.

Use the Buddy System: When in doubt – bring a friend! There's nothing that says self-care has to happen independently, all the time. The next time you want to try a new activity, think about asking one of your friends to come along.

Monthly Review: As you try new things and build your own personalized self-care routine, write down what you like and what you dislike about your current routine so you can further refine your personal routine.

In the Next Chapter

In the next chapter, we'll talk about how seeking professional support is not a sign of weakness but a courageous step towards healing. We'll talk about how finding a therapist or counselor you connect with and who understands your journey can guide you on your journey to long-term sobriety.

Your Self-Care Plan (Part 1: Brainstorm)

Here are a few questions and a list of self-care ideas that you can map into your daily, weekly and monthly routines. Answer each question, then write down how you implement at least one of the activities into your daily, weekly and monthly routine.

Questions to Personalize Your Self-Care Plan

1. What activities make me feel recharged, joyful and overall content with myself?

2. How much time can I realistically dedicate to my self-care on a daily, weekly and monthly basis?

3. Are there new self-care practices I want to learn more about? If so, what?

_____

_____

_____

_____

_____

_____

_____

4. How can I create a balanced self-care plan that allows me to feed myself physically, emotionally, intellectually and spiritually?

_____

_____

_____

_____

_____

_____

_____

Daily Self-Care Activities:

Meditation: Try starting your day with meditation, maybe 2-5 minutes a day. If you find it difficult to close your eyes during meditation, try sitting quietly and observing the world around you, or finding a guided meditation on YouTube.

Write What You're Grateful For: Write 3-5 things you're grateful for when you're having your morning coffee or tea, preferably outside or in a quiet environment. Write about the little things you're grateful for along with larger, big ticket items.

Sunrise Salutations: Try connecting with your body with some morning sunrise salutations (a yoga flow) or some slow stretches.

H2O to Go: Drink a glass of water at the beginning of your day, first thing. When we hydrate our bodies we're more capable of tackling our day!

No Phone Zone: At least an hour before bed, put away your phone and try other ways to unwind before bed.

I can incorporate at least one of these activities in my daily routine in the following ways:

_____

_____

_____

_____

_____

_____

This activity can happen at these following time slots:

Name of Activity:			
Suggested Time #1:			
Suggested Time #2:			

Weekly Self-Care Activities:

Connect with Nature: Spend some time outdoors, walking in a park or by the water, to clear your mind and reconnect with nature. Try to not use your phone during this time to make it more intentional but feel free to listen to some music.

Get Creative: Allocate an hour a week to engage in a creative hobby, like painting, writing, or playing an instrument. Bonus points if you try to incorporate your creative activity at least three times per week.

Self-Care Bath: Enjoy a relaxing bath with Epsom salts, essential oils, a facemask, or some bath bombs. Create a bath that's personalized to you so if that's bringing snacks or Netflix into the mix, feel free!

Connect with Friends: Connecting with friends and family can be an excellent way to unwind at the end of your day. Try having a light-hearted call with friends or family.

Check In On Your Emotional Well-Being: Journal about how you are feeling. Free-write all the disorganized thoughts that come through your head and get it onto paper. Check on your suitcase. Cry it out. Is there something new there you need to process that you didn't really notice was added?

I can incorporate at least one of these activities in my weekly routine in the following ways:

_____

_____

_____

_____

_____

_____

This activity can happen at these following time slots:

Name of Activity:			
Suggested Time #1:			
Suggested Time #2:			

Monthly Self-Care Activities:

Self-Reflection Retreat: Set aside a day of pampering for personal reflection, goal setting, and relaxation. Prep for this day by writing down what you'd like to do, accomplish or how you'd like to relax. You can also incorporate the "Spa Day at Home" as part of your personal "self-reflection retreat."

Spa Day (At Home): Remember in my self-care story where I chose to pamper myself with a nice bath? Try creating an at-home spa experience using candles, face masks or whatever makes you feel pampered and well cared for.

A Day of Adventure: Research a new activity that excites you and plan a day where you do that activity if not several activities. This can include completing a new hike, visiting a museum or trying out a new class.

____ **Club:** Join or start a club of your choice to explore new stories and ideas while socializing. Think of different things you're interested in like a certain tv show, artwork or type of activity that might seem well suited for a group or club environment.

Give Back: Spend a day giving back to a cause that's close to your heart. This can involve helping feed the homeless, volunteering at an animal shelter or finding another way to give back to those less fortunate than you.

I can incorporate at least one of these activities in my monthly routine in the following ways:

_____

_____

_____

_____

_____

_____

This activity can happen at these following time slots:

Name of Activity:			
Suggested Time #1:			
Suggested Time #2:			

Your Self-Care Plan (Part 2: Personalize)

Now that you have some ideas on how you can implement these daily, weekly and monthly self-care exercises, let's use a few pages to map out each activity during the days of the week.

Example:

Daily Routine Schedule:	Kate's Week Day Self-care Schedule
Morning Activity:	Have my coffee and journal 3 gratitudes.
Midday Activity:	Eat my lunch outside, try 5 minutes of silent meditation.
Evening Activity:	One hour before bed, I'll stop using my phone and quiet my mind.

Daily Routine Schedule:	
Morning Activity:	
Midday Activity:	
Evening Activity:	

Weekly Routine Schedule:	
Morning Activity:	
Midday Activity:	
Evening Activity:	

Monthly Routine Schedule:	
Morning Activity:	
Midday Activity:	
Evening Activity:	

References:

Kim, S. C., Sloan, C., Montejano, A., & Quiban, C. (2021). Self-care practices among healthcare professionals: A cross-sectional study. *Journal of Clinical Nursing*, 30(17-18), 2654–2666.

Professional Help (Is Not for the Weak)

ASKING FOR HELP IS NOT GIVING UP. IT'S REFUSING TO GIVE UP.

-CHARLIE MACKESY

We All Need Help Sometimes

Let's go out on a limb and imagine you're suddenly a rock-climbing enthusiast. Kudos to you if you already are. You're on a climb and you slipped and became wedged between two rocks. You're completely stuck and need to call out for help. Of course, you are super safe and you always go with a climbing group, and they're within earshot. You just started climbing with this group and they're all much more advanced. They're always pushing your limits and you feel like if you call out for help, the overwhelming pang of guilt and embarrassment might lead you to never climb with this group again.

Another 15 minutes pass and your leg is now dead asleep and you still haven't figured out how to get out alive all by yourself. One of the climbers yells, "hey, you okay down there?" You pause and take a deep breath – "Actually, yeah I'm stuck, I need some help, can you come down?" They shimmy down and give you a warm smile, "The same thing happened to me on my first big climb, it's no big deal. Try moving your foot this way." A few more maneuvers and you're free and climbing up to the next rest stop where the rest of the group is waiting. When they see you, you're greeted with smiles and a few congratulatory claps. You then realize, asking for help is a hidden, underrated strength, and that really, all anyone wants for you is to see you do well.

Asking For Help

For centuries, women have been brushed off, kept quiet and made to feel like their feelings didn't matter, which is a load of BS. We are worthy of all of the care, attention and stature as our male counterparts. We deserve to be paid attention to and included, our ailments deserve scientific research, and our minds deserve support.

Okay… so let's clear your mind. Tell me exactly what flashes in your mind when you think of the word "strength." If you're anything like me or the rest of the human population, you might have thought of someone with tons of muscles, Superman (better yet, Superwoman), or another type of brave, muscle-y figure. More often than not, we think of the *literal vision of strength* instead of its lowkey cousins – forgiveness and asking for help.

The reality is that asking for help is the internal version of physical strength, and it can be even more challenging for us women when society has been telling us to stay quiet and look pretty. Asking for help, in instances that are especially uncomfortable, pushes us to be vulnerable and honest with both ourselves and the person we're asking to help us. That being said, it takes a great deal of courage and inner strength to bring awareness to the things we need help with so that we can learn from and overcome our obstacles. The incredible thing is that once you open your mind up to asking for help, you will find that there is so much of it out there that is available to you.

The Benefits of Professional Support

One of the key roles of therapists is to treat the root causes of addiction in a safe, confidential, non-judgemental space. Therapists are trained to offer empathy and support every step of your journey so that you can get in touch with and heal your inner child. A recent study conducted in Oakland, California by Cummings et al. (2003) highlights the importance of therapy, noting that patients who consistently spoke to a therapist felt more understood and supported which allowed them to engage more openly and vulnerably. Since they felt that they could express themselves in a safe space, they were more willing to confront their addiction issues and therefore more successful in overcoming them.

My First Therapist Sucked

Alcohol toyed with me for years, but all in all I never had a healthy relationship with alcohol (or weed, or food, or my body…). I was just shy of 22 when my college boyfriend died and I checked out to say the least. My boss at the time strongly encouraged me to go see her therapist and I couldn't have hated it more. She was the kind of therapist who sat back in her chair, her pointer and middle fingers on her cheekbone, ring finger on her lip and thumb under her chin. She stared at me and hardly said a word. It drove me absolutely insane. I was in a place where tears came out of my eyes faster than words out of my mouth and all she could say was "what's going on for you right now, Kate?" That was her response to everything I said. It was worthless. Oh, and she recommended AA. (We will talk more about AA and my thoughts on it in a later chapter). I honestly think she had no idea what to do with me.

You're probably wondering why I am telling you a horror story about going to therapy when the point of this chapter is to convince you to open your mind (if it isn't already) to it and understand that it is an incredibly useful way to learn how to maintain your sobriety. It is because therapy is a bit like dating. You have to try a few therapists in order to find one that really rocks your world. I did find one who turned my world around and she was a tell-it-like-it-is, matter-of-fact, solutions-oriented, prim and proper, never-had-a-problem-herself-so-what-the-heck-is-she-doing-in-addiction-counseling-and-how-is-she-doing-such-a-good-job-at-it, saint. I tracked her down on Facebook at four years sober to tell her so and she called me on the phone to tell me she wasn't allowed to engage with me on social media, but that she was so happy I was doing well and that she played such a huge role in literally saving my life. I can't recommend this kind of connection highly enough.

I just recently started seeing a new therapist and lucky me, she is pretty great too. This time it isn't to focus on addiction, but on past trauma, which if I'm being honest, is 100% related.

Developing Your Coping Strategies

Not only does therapy open the conversation about the root causes of your addiction but it also helps to hone in on coping strategies that work best for you. Let's say you're struggling to handle cravings, stress and triggers when it comes to your drug or drink of choice. Therapy is not just someone throwing down the safety rope to help you up the cliff, but the person shimmying down telling you exactly where to put your feet and hands so you can climb up the mountain yourself. I know it sounds cheesy but it's true. Just like this book, therapy helps you learn an array of tools that you can use by yourself to get you through one day after another without picking up that drink or drug.

Keep in mind that no one is going to simply "save you" from yourself – it's gotta be you who brings it home. You are the one who'll hone your skills and coping strategies over time. You are the one who will try a tool and and talk it out with your therapist about whether or not it worked for you, if you need to tweak it, or if that one simply doesn't resonate with you and you need to move on to the next option. When I realized it was actually possible for me to learn how to get and stay sober and live a happy life if I learned and implemented the right tools, it brought me so much hope. I had felt hopeless for a very long time.

Providing Perspective

Like I mentioned above, therapists provide a different perspective to many inner child wounds that we don't know what to do with, or even know are there. Therapists are able to challenge and bring to light self-destructive patterns and biased thoughts that we never even realized were limiting us. Therapists act as a baseline for us and are there to compassionately question what beliefs we might want to shed about ourselves, others and our environment.

It's okay to not be okay as long as you are not giving up.
- Karen Salmansohn

You've Relapsed, Now What?

You might feel the sharp sting of simply thinking about relapsing and *that's perfectly normal,* especially considering your addiction might have been very close to burning down your entire life, if not succeeding in doing so. Another silver lining of therapy is that your therapist is there for you *no matter what.* Even if you think you have the most gruesome, awful, disgusting experience that you're absolutely horrified with, chances are your therapist has heard it before, if not an even worse version. They're not there to ask you in a judgemental tone, "How could you let this happen?!" They're simply there to help you evaluate, pick up the pieces and create a plan to move forward. Creating a relapse prevention plan can also help you avoid relapsing again by identifying potential triggers, outlining different strategies to avoid high-risk scenarios and having boundary phrases at the ready for when you do feel challenged.

Meet Sara

So let's look at what a relapse prevention plan might look for someone struggling with addiction, specifically when it comes to her first family gathering since being sober:

Background: Sara is a 35-year-old recovering from alcohol dependency and she's been sober for 9 months (freaking amazing!). The holidays are just around the corner and she's told her therapist that she's feeling anxious about seeing her family, especially since Christmas with her family largely involves drinking. Since she's divulged this to her therapist several months in advance, they've been able to come up with a plan to help Sara navigate her family gathering.

Key Components of Sara's Plan:

1. **Emotional Preparation**

    Sara has practiced specific mindful exercises with her therapist and on her own for several months to manage anxiety and stress in real time. She's also written several affirmations on her phone to reinforce her commitment to her sobriety.

2. **Social Strategies**

    Sara has opted to bring a sober friend to her holiday gathering, one of her closest childhood friends. Sara's friend, Joy, understands her journey with sobriety and is there to offer immediate encouragement and support if things become too overwhelming.

3. **Environmental Control**

    Before the event, Sara also spoke to her family members, sending out a group text about how she's decided to stop drinking alcohol. By opening up this conversation, Sara has also set her family's expectations and a firm boundary around alcohol.

4. **Exit Strategy**

    In case things get edgy, Sara's created a clear exit plan that includes her signaling to her sober friend and saying something like "hey, did you remember to feed your cat before we left?" indicating that she's had enough and needs to head home, or at least take a break and regroup – with her friend's support of course.

Outcome:

Sara and her friend Joy end up going to the Christmas party and although there is alcohol aplenty, Sara goes for some sparkling water. Sara did encounter several triggers, one including a distant family member Sara didn't include in the message that offered her a glass of wine at dinner. Sara played the tape forward and said "no". There was also a heated debate about politics after dinner which would usually cause Sara to drink so she could tune it out, but instead she used one of her mindfulness exercises to manage her anxiety real-time. Sara used her exit strategy towards the end of the get together when she saw that many of her family members were already quite drunk and trying to force her into a sloppy dance party. Overall, Sara was proud of herself and felt great the next morning after a good night's sleep.

What happens when people open their hearts? They get better.
- Haruki Murakami

Self Help and Self-care

Like we talked about in Chapter 7, self-care plays a pivotal role in your long-term sobriety success and works hand in hand with seeking professional help. More often than not, many techniques implemented in your self-care routine like meditation, journaling and self reflection are also tools that therapists use to help you control your environment when situations get tense.

Key Takeaways:

Seeking Help Is Brave: It takes a lot of courage to seek help and be honest with yourself about your addiction. Seeking professional support is an act of strength, not a weakness.

Make a Plan: By creating a relapse prevention plan with your therapist, you empower yourself to make better choices when faced with a triggering situation. You can also work with your therapist to create personalized coping strategies to further help you in your day-to-day life and commitment to long-term sobriety.

Finding the Root Cause: One key benefit of allowing yourself to be vulnerable with a therapist is that it allows you to find the root causes of your drinking by critically looking at your inner trauma.

Action Items:

Much like you did in *The Community Challenge* in Chapter 3, we're going to add on to those skills and connections by applying this specifically to professional help and local support groups.

Research Local Groups: Find several different local therapists that you can try and that are financially comfortable for you. Make a note to say what you liked about each local therapist at first glance.

Evaluate Your Options: As you research different therapists in the area, consider their specific qualifications, treatment philosophies and if they specifically deal with addiction and alcohol recovery cases.

Make the Connection: Book a session with each therapist and after meeting with each of them, decide which therapist you'd like to move forward with (remember, it's like dating). After each session with each different therapist, make notes of what you liked, disliked and how you could visualize yourself making progress with this therapist.

In the Next Chapter

In the next chapter we'll compare our relationship with our addiction with an unhealthy partnership. We'll also talk about how a real-life breakup can trigger a relapse and how to manage your triggers within that scenario.

Reflection Questions

Reflection Questions:

What are some of your main goals when it comes to seeking professional help? Write down three main goals that you want to get out of seeing a therapist.

1. _____

_____

_____

_____

_____

_____

_____

2. _____

_____

_____

_____

_____

_____

_____

3. _____

_____

_____

_____

_____

_____

_____

Visualize meeting your therapist for the first time – how do you feel? Are you anxious, excited, hopeful, skeptical? Afterwards, visualize that you've been attending therapy with this therapist for quite some time, how have your feelings changed? What have you noticed about your difference in lifestyle or how you approach triggers? Write down how you feel below.

Before meeting my therapist I feel:

_____

_____

_____

_____

_____

_____

_____

_____

_____

After attending therapy for quite some time I feel:

_____

_____

_____

_____

_____

_____

_____

_____

CBT Visualization – What If?

In this short Cognitive Behavioral Therapy exercise, we'll visualize a few scenarios that might take place at a family gathering. Below you'll visualize a common scenario, how you'd handle a potential trigger and how you feel after you've successfully managed that trigger.

Example:

A distant family member offers me a glass of wine at dinner.	I put my hand over my glass and say "no thank you" and they move on and keep talking about their latest ski trip.	I feel proud of myself for saying "no" and I look over at my partner who gently pats my thigh under the table.

Scenario	Positive Outcome	I Feel…
Your especially rowdy uncle asks you to take a shot with them at a family gathering.		
You're offered a drink from a family friend at a holiday function.		
One of your cousins asks you to "taste this" and it's a glass of wine.		

References:

Cummings, J. R., Allen, L., Clennon, J., McGuffin, P., & Prince, M. (2003). The role of therapeutic alliance in substance abuse treatment outcomes. *Journal of Substance Abuse Treatment*, 24(2), 123-129.

Breakups, Trauma, Sobriety, Oh My!

YOU CAN'T START THE NEXT CHAPTER OF YOUR LIFE IF YOU KEEP RE-READING THE LAST ONE.

-MICHAEL MCMILLAN

The Toxic Ex

Imagine your addiction to alcohol or drugs is that toxic ex that simply won't leave you alone. Talking to them is like walking on a tightrope in crazy-town and you've already blocked their phone number but now they've found your Facebook profile and are sending you lengthy messages filled with nonsense... and you're embarrassed to say you used to fall for it. Despite your best friend's earnest warnings, you'd relapse hard on false promises of comfort, that they won't hurt you as bad as they did last time, that they've changed and you'll be just like every other normal couple who can drink like everyone else if you just give them one last try. But every time is worse than the last, and finally you are fed up with their bullshit. Now, equipped with your tools to keep turning them down with confidence, you have the strength to leave them behind for good.

Even if you're ready to move on, it doesn't mean they are and they'll most likely make it as difficult as possible to move on as long as they're breathing or at least obsessing about you. Just like your toxic ex in real life, alcohol can mirror the same dynamics as a toxic romantic relationship. So let's review some ways you can best prepare yourself for the first encounter with your ex, post break up.

> *You must make a decision that you are going to move on. It won't happen automatically. You will have to rise up and say, 'I don't care how hard this is, I don't care how disappointed I am, I'm not going to let this get the best of me. I'm moving on with my life.'*
>
> *- Joel Osteen*

Step 1: Recognize the Signs

Chances are you've probably seen a few red flags along the way in your relationship. Maybe at first it was making excuses or rain-checking multiple times when making plans with friends just to get piss drunk by yourself on a Friday night. Or maybe it started with small excuses for bad behavior when you were drunk or the realization you were in a codependent relationship with your addiction. Mix that with the negative long term effects on your health and personal relationships and boom – you've got yourself an isolated, toxic relationship. Now how do you get out?

> *Letting go means to come to the realization that some people are a part of your history, but not a part of your destiny.*
>
> *- Steve Maraboli*

Step 2: The Breakup – Deciding to Let Go

Letting go is all about realizing that some people aren't meant to be lifelong friends or partners – some people are just there to teach us a lesson and then get out of our lives. I think my addiction to alcohol was just that – a toxic ex that eventually taught me a very hard lesson to learn; that I couldn't tune out of my own life and needed to take responsibility for my own actions. There are many ways you can go about your breakup with alcohol or drugs. Let's look at a few below:

Pros and Cons

Let's go back to our pros and cons list from Chapter 1. If this relationship was *really beneficial,* the pros would drastically outweigh the cons. So let's think about what utilization alcohol really has in your life and if it outweighs its negative impacts.

When I wrote this pros and cons list for myself, I realized that I couldn't think of more than one pro when it came to my addiction and it wasn't even a *good* pro. I wrote: *it makes awkward moments with company less awkward because I'm too drunk to really care.* Looking back at that, I realized that I was more than ready to break up with alcohol. To be honest, I actually got a bit angry at myself writing the pros and cons list; there were no pros, just cons and my long-term health and relationships hanging by a thread.

Sift Through the Mind Games

When I first broke up with alcohol I felt like it (my addiction) was playing mind games. Some intrusive thoughts would pop in and say *what if I'm not interesting without alcohol,* others would say *my friends only like me because I'm fun to be around,* and so on and so forth. After a while I realized that I had been gaslighting myself – playing mind games with myself in order to justify my relationship with alcohol. So, when you first break up with alcohol, don't be afraid to really ask yourself: *is this my voice speaking or is it my addiction?*

Write a Goodbye Letter

We'll dive into this more in our exercise below this chapter but consider writing a goodbye letter to your addiction. Write down all the reasons you're ending the relationship and how the relationship made you feel. Do your best to express yourself fully when talking about all of the struggles, shortcomings and pain you felt because you felt drained by this toxic relationship. Explain why you can no longer continue the relationship and finally, say goodbye.

Set Clear Boundaries

When breaking up with your toxic ex, the boundaries are never clear for them, probably because they don't have any to begin with… Yet, that doesn't mean you can't practice your strong boundaries, affirmations and boundary phrases (like we did in Chapter 4). One way you can set clear boundaries from the get-go is not putting yourself in compromising situations like those where you'll run into your ex. Sometimes avoiding the situation all together is better than trying to uncomfortably muddle through. Remind yourself that it won't always be like this and as time goes by, you will be able to manage your triggers real-time in anxiety-inducing situations.

Prepare for Setbacks

It's always good to have a backup plan, just like Sara's preventative plan in Chapter 8. Think of all the ways your ex could possibly come crawling back into your life – via Facebook messenger, showing up at your house, calling you at random times in the middle of the night? Make a list of ways that you could possibly have access to your drug or drink of choice and create a plan that can minimize (if not avoid altogether) these unsavory interactions.

Growth is painful. Change is painful. But nothing is as painful as staying stuck somewhere you don't belong.

- Mandy Hale

Step 3: Starting Over – Learning to Love Yourself

It might sound like one of those "live, laugh, love" home decor towels you see at random AirBnB's but it's true, learning to love yourself is a huge part of breaking up with your toxic ex. Let's be honest – do you think you were your best self with them? Do you feel like you were taking care of yourself, practicing good self-care, positive self talk? Well, if you're not doing that for yourself, there's a very slim chance you'd be able to do all those things and more for someone else, particularly any partner, friend or family member in your life. Much like Chapter 6, we'll focus on writing all the things you loved about yourself before being consumed by addiction. Write about what you loved to do before your relationship with your toxic ex, the positive characteristics you embodied both internally and physically and how you felt on a day-to-day basis.

Some of the things you might include in your note to yourself:

- I love my gummy smile
- Friends really appreciated how thoughtful I was
- I was really good at playing volleyball and would play with a local group every week
- I really loved my borderline too loud laugh when I would hang out with my childhood friends

And so on and so forth…

Sometimes the hardest part isn't letting go but rather learning to start over.

Nicole Sobon

Step 4: Rebuilding Your Life

Now that you've recognized the signs of a toxic ex, broken up with them and realized how many things you were missing out on when you were under the influence of your addiction/toxic ex, it's time to rediscover and rebuild your life. I know this sounds like a daunting task, but you've already broken it down in several different ways, without even knowing it! Remember *The Community Challenge* in Chapter 3? Well, there was a bonus section that was all about different hobbies and ways to rebuild your life. Now, we're going to add on to that by dividing each category of your life both professional and personal to help you rediscover yourself and rebuild your life.

Your Personal Life

Remember the barrels of taffy? Well, that's just like rediscovering yourself. Think back to the hobbies you used to enjoy and discover how you can reincorporate them into your life. For instance, was there a softball team you loved playing with? There's no reason you can't contact them and start playing on a weekly basis again! Vice versa, if you're more of an independent exercise person, you could try your hand at tennis, taking classes at your local community center or start swimming laps at the community pool.

Your Professional Life

Now there might be a lot to unpack here, especially if you used to go out with coworkers to drink after a long day (or on your lunch break, or pour vodka in your water glass on your desk…). If you feel yourself getting anxious in a social situation, remember that you made a choice to not allow your addiction to run your life and that's more important than what anyone thinks. When it comes to such a sensitive topic we often think that *everyone is talking about us* or *everyone is thinking I'm lame because I don't drink anymore* but realistically – everyone's too caught up in their own lives to actively stop what they're doing and think that about you.

Step 5: Visualize and Celebrate Your Freedom

Well done! You've made it this far and you're ready to start romanticizing your life – amazing! This is where the fun stuff comes in. Just like we did in Chapter 5 with the "What If" Game, we'll turn to visualization again, this time staying more on the positive side instead of playing through different negative scenarios.

Sit back and find a comfortable position. Take a few deep breaths and visualize yourself in your new life. A life free from your toxic ex, one where you're putting yourself first and giving all that love, compassion and consideration you truly deserve back into yourself. What does that look like for you? Does it look like drinking water first thing in the morning or waking up a bit earlier for work to go on that morning run? Does it look like heading to the community lap pool after work? How do you feel after you do those actions? For example, when you first dive into the water, it probably feels cool and almost a bit of a shock to the system. You realize that once you hit the water, the work day sheds away and you're able to fully immerse yourself in swimming back and forth, one stroke at a time.

In addition, you should also visualize yourself celebrating all sorts of milestones like the one month mark, the six month mark and how it looks to celebrate your sobriety (or breakup with your toxic ex) with friends and family that love you.

Over time I noticed my visualization of alcohol as the toxic ex evolved on its own. As my strength and love for myself increased, it changed from a bad break up with an abuser I was in love with, to feeling like I was donating a pair of jeans that I used to be in love with to Goodwill. While the jeans (i.e. alcohol) used to make me feel great, they just didn't fit me right any more and every time I wore them it was a bad look for me. Now, it is like a god-awful couch I once puked on that I called the junkers to come haul away and I am so very glad it is finally gone. Good riddance.

Key Takeaways:

Realize Your Toxic Ex Needs to Go: Realize that the toxic relationship you were holding onto was extremely one-sided. Use your pros and cons list to justify the fact that this toxic relationship does not serve you.

Rebuild Your Life: Start to rebuild your life by listing things you loved to do before addiction started to consume your time, energy and effort. To make things easier to tackle, try breaking things down into two categories, your personal life and your professional life.

Relish the Freedom: You should be proud of yourself! You're finally free from your toxic ex, just like that photo of Nicole Kidman after she finally divorced Tom Cruise (go Google it if you don't know what I am talking about). Relish in your freedom and your strength – you did it. Be proud of yourself.

Action Items:

Create a Vision Board: Take magazines or find photos online and create a collage of all the things you want to embody in your sobriety. Do you want to try scuba diving? Join a sports team or start volunteering more? What does your self-care routine look like? Try to use as many vision-specific photos as possible. For example, I'm envisioning my skin-care routine and using aloe vera gel every night on my face. I'm going to look for a skin-care photo that features aloe vera.

Speak Kindly to Yourself: Practice positive self talk in the mirror before you start your morning or nightly routine. Work on saying these affirmations to yourself everyday and see how it changes how you see yourself.

Try Something New: Try a new class, hobby or activity you've always wanted to try but seemed just a little out of your comfort zone. Be brave and allow yourself to be imperfect at something new. You may love it!

In the Next Chapter:

In the next chapter, we'll break down the biochemical mechanisms underlying addiction and focus on practicing self-compassion. We'll talk about how overcoming addiction is filled with ups and downs but it's how we can treat ourselves with kindness that makes all the difference.

The Goodbye Letter

Write a goodbye letter to your toxic ex – addiction. Write down all the reasons you're ending the relationship and how the relationship made you feel. Do your best to express yourself fully when talking about all of the struggles, shortcomings and pain you felt because you were drained by this toxic relationship. Explain why you can no longer continue the relationship and finally, say goodbye.

_____

_____

_____

_____

_____

_____

_____

_____

_____

_____

_____

_____

_____

_____

_____

_____

_____

Goodbye, I won't miss you.

X_____

The Chemical Hijack of Compassion

MY RECOVERY MUST COME FIRST SO THAT EVERYTHING I LOVE IN LIFE DOES
NOT HAVE TO COME LAST.

-ANONYMOUS

The Chemical Hijack

The brain is an incredibly powerful organ. The more we understand how it works, the more we can empower ourselves to take back control of our lives when it comes to our addictions and overall compulsions.

As far as addictions in particular are concerned, there are three areas of our brain that are most affected. Our basal ganglia, extended amygdala and prefrontal cortex are all "hijacked" by drugs and alcohol. To put it simply, drugs and alcohol literally take control of our movements, motivation, experiences of reward, the ability to organize thoughts and activities, prioritize tasks, manage time, make decisions, control our behavior, emotions, impulses, and they deregulate our body's response to stress and anxiety. Drugs and alcohol send us into a powerful chemical loop where one area says to another, "this feels good, send more" and then the area responsible for making decisions gets taken over and says, "sure, why not?" until one day it gets to a stage where drinking or using feels essential to our survival, whether it makes us feel good or not (Office Of The Surgeon General 2016).

Prolonged substance abuse can also alter the brain's structure and function, making recovery even more difficult to achieve as your brain tells you that you *need* your fix, especially if you've been dependent on that substance for so long (Kalivas & Volkow 2011). A study by Blum (2012) also explains how some of these cravings and addictions are often linked to genetics, affecting the brain's neurochemistry and development of addictive behaviors more so in some people than in others.

What does this all mean? It means that while you do need to step back and take responsibility for your actions, you can take comfort in the fact that you were truly and most certainly *not yourself* when you went off on your aunt and called her an effing c-word at Thanksgiving 2023. You were sick and your brain chemistry was all out of whack. The good news? Your brain will repair itself over time as you abstain from drugs and alcohol. It will heal and you can, without a doubt, get back in the driver's seat (and send flowers to your aunt).

This brings me to the next point I want to make. You have been sick. Your body and mind have been battered by powerful neurotransmitters gone amuck, and you deserve to be cared for and nursed back to health just like anyone else who is critically ill. Many people will not see it this way, because there is a stigma against addiction, but what matters is that you do, so you can give yourself the tender loving care you need in order to find lasting sobriety.

Self-compassion is simply giving the same kindness to ourselves that we would give to others.

- Christopher Germer

Let me play a little scenario for you:

It's your first day of your new job. Not just any job, *your dream job,* the start of your career and your path to the top of the food chain. Needless to say you're a ball of excitement and anxiety, slowly sweating through your button-up blouse and black trousers. You check your watch, *the train is late,* you think to yourself as you start to bite your nails. You glance up at the sign as the intercom dings. "N Judah Outbound delayed 55 minutes," it squeaks nonchalantly from the loudspeaker. You curse so loud it'd make your grandmother roll over in her grave.

"I knew I should have — UGH I'm so f*** stupid, I can't believe I'm going to be late…" this grumbling goes on for about 10 minutes as you rush to try and call a Lyft instead. You're mentally kicking yourself in the pants until finally you arrive in the Financial District of San Francisco. You see the elevator but push past several people because you think *well it's just going to take too long,* right before you start sprinting up two flights of stairs until you reach the front office. You're in an awful mood on your first day and chastise yourself for every single thing you did wrong or imperfect on your first day. When you get home, you think to yourself how your new coworkers and boss probably already hate you and how you might as well just give up now.

Okay, now let's rewind and try again, this time adding a little bit of compassion to the mix: It's your first day of your new job, the job you'd applied for several times over the past few years and finally, you're ready for your first day. You put on your favorite blouse, some sleek trousers and your signature stilettos, saying your positive affirmations in the mirror before you head out the door. As you stand at the train station, you notice the train's running late, only to hear the loud speaker say the same. "55 minutes late?!" you think to yourself – you're about to lose it when you remember – you deserve the same compassion and kindness you show your friends and family. You take a breath and pat yourself on the hand, "It's not your fault girlfriend, let's call a cab." You end up just getting a cab in time and arrive in the Financial District five minutes before 9am. You think to yourself "Wow, I'm really lucky today," just as the elevator dings and you hop in. You smile at the person next to you and compliment their bag. They get off on the same floor and then you realize – it's your new boss! You go through your first day doing your best and making a few mishaps along the way but that's to be expected while you learn – *you're doing great,* you tell yourself. Finally you head home where you treat yourself to some take out because you know what – you deserve it!

The greatest glory in living lies not in never falling, but in rising every time we fall.

- Nelson Mandela

Compassion in Recovery

Now that we know we have all of these chemical predispositions working against us, we must remember to use our hidden superpower – self compassion (i.e. tender loving care for ourselves). Just like the two scenarios above, having a little self compassion can go a long way. Much like self visualization allows you to manifest in real life what you see in your mind's eye, self compassion has the ability to shift your mindset into that brighter future as well. This is especially critical when understanding your addiction and how it's not that you're simply "weak willed" or any other self-limiting belief. Understand that addiction is (sadly) an extremely common and deathly disease, not a personal moral failing. Once we strip away the guilt and self-limiting beliefs around our addiction, we can break the stigma, shed our baggage and build a more well-rounded, overall better quality of life. So, how do we do that? One great way to start is with daily positive affirmations. Similar to your boundary phrases or your affirmations when you encounter a trigger, you can use these affirmations to build your confidence and cultivate compassion within yourself. I recommend using an EFT (emotional freedom technique), which we'll dive into below, while doing these affirmations. You can also look at yourself in the mirror and say your daily affirmations. Here are fifteen positive statements to help get you started:

Daily Affirmations

1. I am worthy of a healthy and sober lifestyle.

2. Each day I choose my happiness over my habits.

3. I am stronger than my struggles and much braver than my fears.

4. My journey towards recovery is filled with strength and hope.

5. I am in charge of how I feel today and I choose my happiness and health over cravings.

6. I release the past so I can live fully in the present moment.

7. Every step forward in my sobriety is a victory.

8. I am deserving of respect, love and a joyous life.

9. I am proud of myself and the courage/compassion I show myself every day.

10. My sobriety is a testament to my strength and commitment to myself.

11. I am enough and each day in recovery I grow stronger.

12. I trust my own ability to unlock the path to my own well-being.

13. With each sober breath, I actively build a brighter and healthier future for myself.

14. I embrace my power to stay strong against any challenges that addiction brings.

15. Today, I choose to love myself and celebrate my sobriety.

As you practice your affirmations feel free to create some that are more curated to you. We'll also focus on doing this in the exercise below.

The Chemical Hijack – The EFT Advantage

Let's talk about how we can use the chemical hijack to our advantage – specifically by using EFT, also known as the *Emotional Freedom Technique*. This technique is used by health professionals world-wide, specifically for healing different kinds of trauma. EFT can help our daily affirmations really sink in.

What Is EFT and How it Helps

EFT is an emotional freedom technique that uses physically "tapping" different parts of your body to effectively manage emotions and reduce stress (Purdue University, 2023). When combined with affirmations, EFT can help reinforce the positive belief systems you're verbally telling yourself, making those affirmations even more psychologically impactful. Think of the tapping as muscle memory. Every time you tap your collarbone (for example) and say your affirmations in front of the mirror, you're further solidifying that belief in your brain. After a while, muscle memory kicks in and you inherently think of the positive affirmations you were consistently feeding yourself. The physical tapping of EFT is done on different meridians (or energy points) around the body to calm the nervous system and reduce the overall emotional intensity around negative thoughts; further encouraging your brain to accept those positive affirmations.

The History and Science Behind EFT

EFT has been around for decades and has been used both by western and eastern medicine practitioners. It was first used by practitioners of traditional Chinese medicine, who would map and follow a network of energetic pathways (Qi, pronounced "chee") within the body. EFT is related to acupuncture which involves pressing key points with small needles, along the body's meridians to cure a variety of ailments.

In a study conducted by Church, D., Yount, G., & Brooks, A.J. (2012), researchers found that there were significant changes in cortisol (stress) levels along with different psychological trauma symptoms when performing EFT (as opposed to having zero treatment.) Further supporting the fact that integrating these tapping methods can work with modern psychology practices when overcoming anxiety, depression, addiction and PTSD.

Understanding the EFT Points

The Emotional Freedom Technique requires you to continuously tap on specific points on the body that correspond with meridians. These meridians act as natural intersection points of your body or "hot spots" that can help you balance your energy and reduce overall physical/emotional discomfort.

Basic EFT Points

Here are some of the basic EFT tapping points you can use when performing your affirmations.

- **Top of the Head (TH):** Center of the skull.
- **Eyebrow (EB):** Just at the beginning of the eyebrow, near the bridge of the nose.
- **Side of the Eye (SE):** On the bone bordering the outside corner of the eye.
- **Under the Eye (UE):** On the bone under an eye about 1 inch below your pupil.
- **Under the Nose (UN):** Between the bottom of the nose and the upper lip.
- **Chin (CH):** Midway between the point of your chin and the bottom of your lower lip.
- **Beginning of the Collarbone (CB):** The junction where the sternum (breastbone), collarbone, and the first rib meet.
- **Under the Arm (UA):** On the side of the body, about four inches below the armpit.

How to Tap

- **Use Your Fingers:** Use your fingers to gently tap with the tips of your index and middle finger. It should be firm but not excessively hard.
- **Tap Each Point 5-7 Times:** Tap 5-7 times with your fingertips and an even, rhythmic pace to get the most out of this exercise.
- **Breath Normally:** Breath normally as you recite your affirmations and use EFT to solidify your new mantras.

Practical Application

In the activity below, I'll show you how to incorporate EFT tapping into your affirmation routine, let's begin!

1. **Pick an Affirmation:** Choose one affirmation to continuously repeat. This is important because this activity works best if the statement (your affirmation) and the action (the tapping) is done consistently.

2. **Choose a Meridian:** Choose a meridian (tapping area) from the list above and begin saying your affirmations and tapping. Run through two cycles of these, each around 5-7 taps per each cycle. Remember to take your time and tap at a comfortable, rhythmic pace.

3. **Progress Through Different Points:** Choose two other tapping points to incorporate, saying the same affirmation throughout all points. Repeat at least once per day with the same affirmation for at least one to two weeks.

4. **Reflect and Repeat:** Note the changes in mindset you experience after completing the exercise daily for several weeks. Reflect and choose a new affirmation to repeat the process with.

Every worthy act is difficult. Ascent is always difficult. Descent is easy and often slippery.

- Mahatma Gandhi

Key Takeaways:

Use Your Brain to Your Advantage: Rewire your brain using the EFT methods and positive affirmations as outlined above. This way you can better break the cycle of addiction.

Choose Compassion: Would you talk to a close friend the way you talk to yourself? If not, then something needs to change. We often forget that we're just as worthy of compassion as our friends, family members, neighbors, etc…

Practical Application: Put everything you've learned in this chapter into action by consistently practicing the affirmations and EFT method each day. Reflect at the end of the two week period to see how much your mindset has changed. I know it may seem kind of "out there", but trust me, don't knock it before you try it!

Action Items:

Daily Affirmations: Say your affirmations daily and choose one affirmation to complete with your daily EFT tapping exercise outlined on the previous page under "Practical Application".

In the Next Chapter:

In the next chapter, we'll talk about the elephant in the room – AA and specifically why I hated it at first, and then how it eventually saved my life. We'll also explore different pathways to recovery and support and how to find the right fit for you, whether it's AA, therapy, self-help literature or a mix of a few methods, which is ideal.

From Negative to Positive

In this exercise we'll challenge our negative thoughts and replace them with empowering beliefs. The more you curate your affirmations to fit you, specifically, the easier it is to believe and rewire your brain into believing them! Take each negative affirmation and write a corresponding positive statement that breaks the negative self-limiting belief. Use the extra space below to write your own limiting beliefs that you'll transform into positive affirmations.

Example:

Self-Limiting Belief	Positive Affirmation
I can't do anything right, I'm a failure.	*I might not get things perfect on the first try but I always try again. I am resilient, intelligent and have accomplished many of my long and short term goals.*
I can't handle stress without alcohol.	*I am capable of managing my stress with healthy coping mechanisms that nourish both my mind and my body.*
I'm not strong enough to stay sober.	*I am not only strong but I'm resilient. I choose to not give up on myself because I am worthy of a life that I love. I am fully equipped to maintain my sobriety.*
Relapse is basically me failing myself, again.	*I know within each challenge is a lesson to be learned. I let go of my self guilt and baggage so I can compassionately step into the future.*

People will think I'm no fun without alcohol.	*My friends and family love me for who I am without alcohol. I am naturally interesting, fun and people love being around me. My true personality shines brightly, especially when I'm sober.*
People won't accept me when I'm sober.	*The right people will always love and accept me for who my true, authentic self is.*
I've damaged my relationships beyond repair.	*Sobriety gives me a second chance to build stronger relationships with those I love.*
Sobriety is boring.	*Because I'm sober, I can try new hobbies, passions and interests to improve my life.*
I don't deserve to be happy or sober.	*I deserve a life filled with good health, happiness and sobriety.*

Keep going:

Self Limiting Belief	Positive Affirmation

References:

Blum, K., Werner, T., Carnes, S., Carnes, P., Bowirrat, A., Giordano, J., ... & Gold, M. S. (2012). Sex, drugs, and rock 'n' roll: Hypothesizing common mesolimbic activation as a function of reward gene polymorphisms. *Journal of Psychoactive Drugs*, 44(1), 38-55.

Church, D., Yount, G., & Brooks, A. J. (2012). The effect of emotional freedom techniques on stress biochemistry: A randomized controlled trial. *Journal of Nervous and Mental Disease*, 300(8), 891-896.

Heilig, M., Goldman, D., Berrettini, W., & O'Brien, C. P. (2011). Pharmacogenetic approaches to the treatment of alcohol addiction. *Nature Reviews Neuroscience*, 12(11), 670-684.

Kalivas, P. W., & Volkow, N. D. (2011). New medications for drug addiction hiding in glutamatergic neuroplasticity. *Molecular Psychiatry*, 16(10), 974-986.

Marlatt, G. A., & Donovan, D. M. (Eds.). (2011). *Relapse prevention: Maintenance strategies in the treatment of addictive behaviors.* Guilford Press.

Substance Abuse and Mental Health Services Administration (US), O. O. T. S. G. (2016). The neurobiology of substance use, misuse, and addiction. *Facing Addiction in America: The Surgeon General's Report on Alcohol, Drugs, and Health* [Internet].

Alcoholics Anonymous And Why It Is Or Isn't For You

ONE SIZE DOES NOT FIT ALL: ONE TYPE OF THERAPY OR ONE TYPE OF
MEETING COULD NEVER, EVER FIT EVERYONE'S NEEDS.

-ANNE M. FLETCHER

Angry Atheist

When I was first getting sober, I came into AA as an angry, fallen Catholic Atheist and relapsed multiple times simply over the fact that God was mentioned or referenced SIX times in the twelve steps. My first *several* meetings, I sat and stared at the poster of the twelve steps hanging on the wall and heard absolutely nothing that was said. Heck, practically the only thing I could read from the poster was G-O-D in flashing lights. I felt like I was seven years old, wearing my Catholic school jumper overhearing my neighbor say she didn't believe in God and my world was collapsing all over again. Whether or not He existed, I was pissed at Him. I tried to find another option to get sober, but what it boiled down to for me was that AA was the most accessible of any recovery community I could find. In San Francisco, you can find multiple meetings any time of day and be around others who will help make sure you don't drink. Being a woman of convenience, I decided to hunker down and make it work for me.

I thought to myself, *well, if so many people have gotten sober using AA then it's worth a shot because the alternative is even worse... It's do or die, Kate... do or fucking die.* The magic happened for me when I met my sponsor. They say to pick one who has what you want and she certainly did. She shared her story about how she and her now husband were super strung out and that now they're both sober and married with three boys. She was one of those magnetic people that everyone wants to be friends with. When I met her, my then-boyfriend and I were trying to claw out of our respective hells… and now we are married and sober, with two boys. She had what I wanted, that's for sure, and because of her, it is mine now too. She helped me interpret the outdated literature, roll my eyes at the sexism, look past it for the sake of saving my life, and come to an understanding of my own higher power (which I will even go so far as to call "God" as a way to sum it up). She is a badass, straight-talking, tatted up mama. She and AA *did* save my life, after all my kicking and screaming about it.

Some people think of AA as a cult, and by definition it arguably is. Some people think AA-goers are brainwashed, and we clap back by saying that maybe our brains needed washing. This chapter is not about convincing you that AA is the way to go, but to help you figure out how to buckle down with a support system that will work for *you*.

Finding Your AA

Although I personally went through the twelve-steps in AA and did grow to love it and appreciate it for saving my life, I do believe that one size does not fit all. That's why I would highly recommend looking into different options to find what speaks to you most. Much like our lives, our journey to long-term sobriety should also be customized to us, and staying sober is often the result of a mixture of many support methods, not just one. I find the more we can identify with the process and our version of the "twelve-step" program, the easier it is for us to visualize ourselves succeeding.

Although we've already outlined finding different types of communities and seeking out different therapists, here we'll explore alternative recovery options and how to find them. Afterwards, we'll put it all together in creating a cohesive plan.

Secular and Therapy-Based Recovery Options:

SMART Recovery (Self-Management and Recovery Training):

SMART recovery uses a science-based approach that includes things like CBT (cognitive behavioral therapy) , something that we also touched upon in Chapter 8 with our CBT "What If" Scenario worksheet. If you find you liked the worksheet and want to focus more on practicalities and self-reliance, SMART recovery might be a good fit for you.

Refuge Recovery:

This program focuses on the mindfulness associated with addiction and their community's practices follow a Buddhist philosophy as the foundation of their recovery process. If you liked our Mindful Moments from Chapter 2's action items or Chapter 7's emphasis on self-compassion, you might like Refuge Recovery's approach to sobriety.

Cognitive Behavioral Therapy (CBT) and Dialectical Behavioral Therapy (DBT):

As said above, cognitive behavioral therapy could be a great option for those looking to go with a more therapy-based approach to recovery. In addition, DBT (Dialectical Behavioral Therapy) was originally focused on treating those with borderline personality disorder but recent studies show it has been effective in treating substance abuse patients as well. This type of therapy focuses on improving emotional regulation techniques, mindfulness and stress management skills. You would need to find therapists who specialize in these techniques if this is an option you'd like to explore.

Online Platforms and Sober Community Support Groups:

Sobriety Sisters:

If you're on Facebook, I can't recommend Sobriety Sisters highly enough. It is a private Facebook group for both women struggling to get and stay sober and women with long term sobriety alike. It has a whopping 58,000 members at the time of writing this book and I see that number increasing every day. I am an active member, so hop on and say hi! You can post anonymously too if you are in need of support and aren't ready to reveal your identity.

Reddit Recovery Communities:

Reddit is an online community of anonymous individuals that has a TON of recovery communities, specifically for different substance abuse and alcohol recovery issues. Although Reddit is **not specifically for alcohol recovery,** it can make for a great addition to your recovery plan.

A quick Google search will get you linked up with any of the options listed above. This list is not exhaustive. There are many resources available to you, so if you stumble on others, add them to the menu of support communities you might want to be a part of.

A Step-by-Step Guide

Step 1: Assess Your Personal Needs and Beliefs

Sit down and evaluate what your personal beliefs, needs and goals are when creating your recovery plan. Feel free to use a "Pros and Cons" type list, similar to what we talked about in Chapter 9, writing down the benefits and negative takeaways for each option.

Step 2: Explore Alternative Options

If you're interested in seeking alternative options, research the communities and alternatives listed above by going to their websites and learning more about each program. Consider the values you outlined in Step 1 to help you access which programs might be a good fit for you.

Step 3: Engage with the Community

Much like *The Community Challenge* we did in Chapter 3 – start attending different meetings both in-person and online to see what you like. Take note of what you liked and disliked. Regularly attend meetings for two weeks (or more) then choose which groups you'd like to move forward with.

Step 4: Build Upon Your Foundation – Your Support Group

As you start to attend more meetings either virtually or in-person, do your best to start creating a network of both recovery group friends, pre-existing supportive friends, family members and others who want you to succeed. When you build your circle full of people who *want to help you,* it's easier to gain confidence and feel like you're not alone in your journey to recovery. Don't be afraid to reach out. Remember, asking for help is a strength, not a weakness.

Step 5: Solidify Your Recovery Plan

After you've found a community and program that works well for you, solidify your plan by consistently attending meetings, showing up virtually or acting in a way that promotes your long-term sobriety. Further curate your recovery plan by incorporating self-care rituals and invest in yourself through your hobbies, healthy social interactions (ideally without your substance of choice ever present) or your self-care plan.

Step 6: Evaluate and Adapt as You Go

Check-in with yourself every few weeks by journaling or simply sitting down and thinking about how you're currently doing, what you like and what you could improve upon. By checking-in with ourselves, we clear our brains of the excess clutter that might be blurring our vision of the big picture. Feel free to also visualize yourself and your next steps in your recovery. For example, in the next two weeks you might want to speak up in your support group at least two times and you envision yourself raising your hand and speaking in front of your group and being positively received by all group members.

Step 7: Embracing the Journey

Sobriety is a marathon and we need to treat it as such. When we embrace the lifelong journey with a curious mind, gratitude and the idea that we'll forever be learning and growing, we can find joy in the present moment instead of simply the end destination.

Questions to Ask Yourself

When Evaluating Recovery Options That Are Not AA

Answer and circle Yes or No for each question below, write a little bit about why you said Yes or No, and find the best option(s) for recovery in the answer key provided at the end.

1. Is it important for you to have a recovery program that's based on scientific principles like Cognitive Behavioral Therapy?

    Yes   No

    _____
    _____
    _____
    _____
    _____
    _____

2. Do you prefer a recovery community that emphasizes self-empowerment, compassion, and self-reliance over other "higher powers"?

Yes   No

_____
_____
_____
_____
_____

3. How do you feel about integrating mindfulness and meditation into your daily recovery process?

Yes   No

_____
_____
_____
_____
_____

4. Does the idea of utilizing Buddhist philosophy as a foundational tool for sobriety resonate with you?

Yes   No

_____
_____
_____
_____
_____
_____

5. Reflecting on the "What If Scenario" CBT exercises in Chapter 8, did you feel this approach helped you manage difficult emotions and situations related to sobriety? How did you feel after you completed the exercise?

Yes   No

_____

_____

_____

_____

_____

6. Do you feel like therapy-based tools allow you to emotionally regulate, relieve stress and increase mindfulness in your day-to-day routine?

Yes   No

_____

_____

_____

_____

_____

7. How comfortable are you with using technology as a medium for recovery? Do you find that online interactions are beneficial and supportive?

Yes   No

_____

_____

_____

_____

_____

8. Would you prefer a virtual platform that offers a variety of recovery methods, including connecting with others online?

   Yes   No

   _____

   _____

   _____

   _____

   _____

9. How do you feel about online forums? Do you feel that anonymous interactions can provide the support you need?

   Yes   No

   _____

   _____

   _____

   _____

   _____

10. Do you like a diverse set of perspectives when it comes to recovery options? Do you think a broad online community can offer valuable insights?

    Yes   No

    _____

    _____

    _____

    _____

    _____

    _____

Finding the Best Option for You

- *If you said Yes to questions 1-2 either both or one of these questions, consider the SMART recovery option.*

- *If you said Yes to questions 3-4 either both or one of these questions, consider the Refuge Recovery option.*

- *If you said Yes to questions 5-6 either both or one of these questions, consider a therapy-based recovery option.*

- *If you said Yes to questions 7-10 either both or one of these questions, consider an online forum (like Reddit) or an application (like SoberGrid).*

Building Your Custom Step-by-Step Guide

Step 1 Questions: Assess Your Personal Needs and Beliefs

What are my core beliefs around sobriety and recovery? How do my own needs align with the beliefs I listed above?

_____

_____

_____

_____

_____

_____

_____

_____

_____

Step 2 Questions: Explore Alternative Options

What are the pros and cons of the current recovery options I'm considering? What do I want to gain from my recovery plan (aside from long-term sobriety) and what potential challenges might lie ahead?

_____

_____

_____

_____

_____

_____

_____

_____

Step 3 Questions: Engage with the Community

After researching different communities and programs, which ones resonate most with my needs and values? What aspects of the programs I listed above stick out to me? Why? What were my first impressions of the groups I attended?

_____

_____

_____

_____

_____

_____

_____

_____

_____

Step 4 Questions: Build Upon Your Foundation – Your Support Group

Who in my current social circle provides the most support for my sobriety journey? (Feel free to list more than one person). What steps can I take to strengthen those relationships and build upon my pre-existing network?

_____

_____

_____

_____

_____

_____

_____

_____

_____

Step 5 Questions: Solidify Your Recovery Plan

How am I showing up for myself in meetings and how have I been engaging in each different community? Am I really trying? Do I need to open my mind to it more?

_____

_____

_____

_____

_____

_____

_____

_____

_____

Step 6 Questions: Evaluate and Adapt as You Go

What have been my little "wins" when it comes to my journey in sobriety? What areas could I possibly improve upon? How have I reached my goals? If not, how can I reach my goals in the future?

_____

_____

_____

_____

_____

_____

_____

_____

_____

Step 7 Questions: Embracing the Journey

How can I cultivate gratitude and remain curious about my sobriety journey? How can I find joy in the present moment and my short-term goals?

_____

_____

_____

_____

_____

_____

_____

_____

_____

_____

Putting it All Together

This book is packed with information and many, many tips to help you get and stay sober, so it's important to remember that it is not to be read only once. As you go back and review certain chapters that spoke to you more loudly than others, you will further cement those suggested strategies into your routine. Things will click for you that didn't the first (or second, or third) time around, and some of them could be the tools that you never knew you needed to keep you from getting drunk and getting behind the wheel next week. Once you have those incorporated into your life, you can go back and look at the chapters that were more like a dull whisper and find that the subtle messages they carried could be what finally gives you the courage to stand up to that person in your life who is not worth the emotional toll they've been taking on you.

Let's do a thorough job. Let's get you sober, keep you sober, and as promised... get you HAPPY.

-Kate

P.S. If you're like me and like looking at a linear timeline of things to stay "on track" with your recovery, here's a suggested 6-week timeline on the next page.

Reminder To Grab Your *BONUSES*

Visit: www.myhappysoberlife.com or scan the QR code so you can download your bonus gratitude journal and start your daily gratitude practice. Also included is a guide to get out of a bad living situation and a guide on getting good sleep in early recovery.

6 Week Timeline

Week 1: Finding the Gratitude Glimmers

- **Days 1-7 (Chapter 1: Gratitude Where There Is None):**
    - Focus: Allow yourself to let go of guilt and find gratitude in the little "glimmers" of life.
    - Exercises: Hash out your pros and cons list and your done list. Start the 3/30 challenge and see how you feel after 30 days!

Week 2: Learning About Mindfulness and Community

- **Days 8-9 (Chapter 2: One Minute at a Time):**
    - Focus: Chip away at your cravings by taking things one minute at a time.
    - Exercise: Use urge surfing to your advantage when the urge to drink arises. Use mindfulness exercises to let go of the past, in order to step into your future.
- **Days 9-14 (Chapter 3: Keep Yourself Occupied – Keep Yourself Alive):**
    - Focus: Actively engage with different sober communities and hobbies.
    - Exercise: Join an online community and attend in person and online sobriety groups.

Week 3: Open Communication and Boundary Setting

- **Days 15-17 (Chapter 4: What to Say to People When You've Stopped Drinking):**
  - Focus: Learn more about your triggers and stick to your boundaries.
  - Exercise: Create boundary phrases to set yourself up for success when being faced with the temptation to drink.
- **Days 18-21 (Chapter 5: Think It Through):**
  - Focus: Visualize the consequences of drinking versus not.
  - Exercise: Use the 3 steps (visualize, breakdown the situation and make a positive choice) to make a decision not only for your present self but your future "you."

Week 4: Letting Go of Guilt and Embracing Self-Care

- **Days 22-24 (Chapter 6: The Suitcase Method – Lightening Your Load):**
  - Focus: Let go of your self guilt as you unpack your emotional suitcase of mistakes and wrong-doings.
  - Exercise: Write a compassionate letter to yourself, forgiving yourself for what you've done in the past so you can step into the future lighter.
- **Days 25-28 (Chapter 7: Permission to Splurge Otherwise):**
  - Focus: Curate your own self-care routine and learn the difference between self-care and self-indulgence.
  - Exercise: Implement self-care practices daily, with sprinkles of self-indulgence.

Week 5: Seeking Professional Help and the Toxic Ex

- **Days 29-31 (Chapter 8: Professional Help Is Not for the Weak):**
  - Focus: Understand that seeking help is not weak but brave.

- Exercise: Review your options when it comes to seeing a health professional.

- **Days 32-35 (Chapter 9: Breakups, Trauma, Sobriety, Oh My!):**
  - Focus: Compare your relationship to alcohol as if it were a toxic ex and realize that your ex needs to go. Start rebuilding your life and relish in the new freedom.
  - Exercise: Create a detailed vision board for your journey through sobriety and write a goodbye letter to your toxic ex.

Week 6: Retraining Your Brain and AA Alternatives

- **Days 36-38 (Chapter 10: The Chemical Hijack of Compassion):**
  - Focus: Understand the biochemical relationship that addiction has on our brains and use EFT and positive affirmations to your advantage.
  - Exercise: Do your personalized daily affirmations coupled with EFT exercises. Break self-limited beliefs with our CBT exercise.

- **Days 39-42 (Chapter 11: Alcoholics Anonymous And Why It Is Or Isn't For You):**
  - Focus: Explore AA and alternatives to AA.
  - Exercise: Take the questionnaire and try AA and several alternatives to AA.

Made in the USA
Columbia, SC
19 November 2024

46942496R00100